STANDARD AMERICAN ENGLISH

STANDARD AMERICAN ENGLISH

ELISABETH HOUSTON

Litmus Press, 2022

ISBN: 978–1–933959–50–4

Cover artwork © Lauren Kelley, *Back Float*, 2006 and *On Ice*, 2007
Design and typesetting by HR Hegnauer

Litmus Press is a program of Ether Sea Projects, Inc., a 501(c)(3) non-profit literature and arts organization. We are dedicated to publishing innovative, cross-genre, and interdisciplinary work by poets, writers, translators, and artists.

Litmus Press publications are made possible by the New York State Council on the Arts with support from Governor Kathy Hochul and the New York State Legislature. Additional support for Litmus Press comes from the Leslie Scalapino – O Books Fund, The Post-Apollo Press, individual members and donors. All contributions are fully tax-deductible.

Library of Congress Cataloging-in-Publication Data:
    Names: Houston, Elisabeth, author.
    Title: Standard American English / Elisabeth Houston.
    Description: Brooklyn, New York : Litmus Press, 2022.
    Identifiers: LCCN 2022009100 | ISBN 9781933959504 (trade paperback)
    Subjects: LCGFT: Poetry.
    Classification: LCC PS3608.O86446 S73 2022 | DDC 811/.6--dc23/eng/20220225
    LC record available at https://lccn.loc.gov/2022009100

Litmus Press
925 Bergen Street, Suite 405
Brooklyn, New York 11238
litmuspress.org

Distributed by Small Press Distribution
1341 Seventh Street
Berkeley, California 94710
spdbooks.org

shhhh

marigolds & honey

(whud mama do?) (mama
do nothin much, she jus
sat & wat-ched & cough
sum-time. sum-time she ride
up & down & up like she
a horsseee.) [*silence. gulp.*]
(u need anee ting from me?)
(aw u so sweet, u so sweet
i could lick u. tho i mus
say i don't tink i need
much of aneting fro u
i jus need u to cum
over here & gimme
a kiss gimme
a kiss.)

the intelligence of grief

(yes/ i am / a dum-dum./ yes, ma-ma/ put me/
away in da closet/ no, der were no/ spank-ins
/ der was silence / & other such tings dat make u
tin-gle - only a lil bit.) (whut such tings?) (oh, tings
like mayo-nn-aise & vas-eo-line & sometimes
my bunnn-eee rabbit na-named ge-eof-freee)
(whut did geofrey say?) (ge-eof-freee say
its all ri-ght, its all ri-ght. chile, you gonna be alright.)

4

advert.

baby likes 2 lick words & dip pencils in tar.
she also likes 2 stuff her pussy w/ feathers
& get w i l d! and crazee. she's up 4 a good
time on sundays & mondays & thursdays.
don't try her fridays b/c she's @ shabbos
dinner w/da hasidim. (the hasidim live
@ 7 maple drive in nyack, new york, you
should stop by if you can. party gets started
around 6 or at least @ sundown. but make
sure to wear a long-ass skirt b/c they like 2
dress real, real proper.)

                              okay?

ps:

oh, yea - and be prepared 4 wigs & fur hats
& a whole lotta singing. i don't know if baby
will sing. you'll have 2 come & find out.

pro-prop-aganda

white castle powder puffs

baby wanted   the kind of diamond   encrusted friendships   celebrities seemed
to have;   madonna   whispered to gwyneth   who tied a red kaballah string around
oprah's wrist, who pulled the levers   of the great capitalist enterprise
cha-cha-cha- cccching!   & made the whole goddamn   world tick
like a finely tuned rolex watch. baby wanted those sort of friends.

she wanted   razzle-dazzle-spinnnnammazzle friends.   she wanted to travel in
a pack of well-coifed girls[1]   whose glamour   would seal her fortune forever,   girls
whose beauty   could erect a fortress   against all she wanted to keep out,
shame &   solitude &   penury &   general freakishness.[2]

baby wanted it easy;   she wanted to luxuriate   in the decadence of high class friends.
she didn't want to toil,   among the   *hhhhhrrrruumppffff!* m-m-m-m-mmmiddle
class,   w. their low-brow tastes,   their knock off bags,   and payless loafers.

... no, she wanted a life   greater than that - she wanted a life bigger.   her
friends,   she was sure,   would seal her fortune.   & so   each night,   she'd rank
her friends in her notebook.   she dreamed   of the perfect combination   of friends

---

1 the girls would all be date raped at age 14, 16 & 21. jenny would also be gang raped, and davida would have a secret affair with her
   lacrosse coach – and while it was "consensual" – before sexual intercourse, he would sit on her head and pour gatorade into her
   vagina, and it would take years of therapy for davida to learn that no, this was not, in fact, "normal" teenage behavior.
2 one day after practice, jenny grabbed davida's hair extensions – pulling on her long black braids – as she screamed "horse hair! horse
   hair!" afterwards, jenny would claim that she'd heard hair extensions could burn quite well and she'd thought they'd make perfect
   flammable material – along with firewood – for the school bonfire that would happen in spring.

& fun & popularity.[3]

& so -   she wrote,

1. jenny
2. lila
3. davida
4. tabitha

or sometimes,

1. jenny
2. davida – lila ??[4]
3. lila – davida??
4. tabitha[5]

& very, very, occasionally

---

3 davida's lacrosse coach was convinced that davida was a "mature girl" and he used such logic to justify humping and pumping the brains out of this very beautiful black girl. since he knew about ida b wells and he'd studied sociology, he was well suited, he surmised, to be davida's very first lover.

4 lila and davida were actually arch-enemies and they'd fought over jenny – for jenny, cruel as she was, stood at the pinnacle of popularity. jenny would play one off the other, sometimes spilling secrets – lila's bulimia, davida's herpes – or other times simply telling tall tales. "davida hates you, lila. you should beat her with a pipe."

5 tabitha was a sweet girl who had a rollicking sex life. jenny got wind of this and wrote an article in the school newspaper, where she stated in clear block print that Miss Tabitha Smiley had slept with fifteen of the football players on the varsity team. she was unaware of the impact of her words nor did she see what lay beneath (ie: *insecurity, jealousy, a fragile ego*) and as a result she continued blindly – and with ferocious intensity – to launch a school wide campaign to expel tabitha smiley from school on account of her "unsavory sexual practices."

1. ???
2. ???
3. ???
4. ??? jenny ???[6]

surprisingly, or not -   baby didn't think of boys.   she didn't think how boys might
figure   into her evil empire; this empire included mostly women &   mostly women
w. impossibly large tits, small waists,   rich fathers,   or rich sugar daddies   and little
else   to their name.

sure, boys figured into   baby's dream   of towering popularity   in so far as
they might catapult   her farther into the castle.   baby wanted to be at the center
of it all   & *suuuuuuuuure*   boys helped.   boys made baby   even more popular
& hot boys   made baby   even more popular.   secretly,   though baby didn't think
much   of boys;   most boys were stupid   & gross & had long schlongs   & often
wanted baby   to do things w. them   baby did not like ...   things like suck & fiddle
& pinch & snap ...   things baby was not   very comfortable w.   and things baby
surely did not tell   lila   or jenny   or davida   or tabitha about ...

it was women who ruled,   it was women   baby wanted: jenny & lila & davida &
tabitha.   there was nothing beyond the horizon   of those four golden girls   -
nothing more: baby could see. she was blinded by want: liposuction & lisa frank
& 400 dollar-bulimia-trained therapists ...   jessica & elizabeth   wakefield

---

6 five months later baby would crumple this list, throw it in the basket & scream at the top of her lungs: "i am done! i am done! i can't
   do jenny lowenberg!" five months later, baby wore clogs, himalayan scarves, and had a girlfriend named lani. she would publicly
   forsake her plastics, her lists, and her obsession with power & privilege and begin to rank, instead, her feminist fairy godmothers –
   hooks, foucault, dworkin, and butler – in various towers of truth.

cavorting around   the cul-de-sac of sunnydale, ca   110 degrees out   climate change
sssssssizzzzzzlinggggg   dis world   dry making martians of us:
making us: alien-ated   franc- ine
pascal   was it
or was it   her ghost

baby eats dog food! or "a diagnosis called suffering"

baby contemplated eating dog food because gwyneth paltrow ate dog food
and she wanted to be skinny – just like gwynnie!
she went to the supermarket late one night
in a fit of nerves[1] & tears[2] & jumping-jack-dreams
so she could buy dog food: so she could nibble on kibble

     – & *not get fat ...*

... what she bought instead was the wet, canned kind,
which she placed at the center of her plate
when she returned home late

& sprinkled some parsley
& dipped in some mayo
& squirted some ketchup...

yum yum yum yum baby said, licking her lips
       & – chomping her bit – *what could be more deeeeelicious*

---

1 yes, baby had psychiatric problems. yes, psychiatry is real. yes, it isn't just pseudo-science. yes, baby took pills because she liked to eat dog food & yes, the author would come to take pills too because she came up with the idea of a baby who liked to eat dog food. it would take the author several trips to the loony bin before she realized that she too needed psych meds. she'd resisted because she didn't want to be *craaaazzzeee* and the very concept of psychiatry seemed to make her *craaaazzzeee*.

2 it would also take baby several trips to the loony bin before she realized she too needed psych meds. it would be just the same with the author. they seemed to live parallel lives, suffer parallel neuroses – *bi-polar & bulimia & occasional fits of OCD* – and psychiatry would be another plot line in the story of baby, another plot line in the story of language.

she picked up her fork,   *"great silver spear it was"* –
and dove it
into the dog food / salad

it landed with a :   *PLUNK!*[3]

m-m-m-m-m-m-m-mmmmmmmmmm
        deeeeeeelicishioussssss[4]   &   *nuttttttrisssshiousssss*

just then, in a flash –

mother scurried into the kitchen & flipped on the lights

        OOOOOOO WWWWEEEEEEEE OOOOOOO WWWWWEEEEEEE[5]

mother didn't like to enter baby stories, mother
didn't like to enter baby rooms,

---

3   the cartoonish elements of the text bore a striking resemblance to baby's favorite childhood television show, ren & stimpee – which aired at 10 am eastern standard time on nickelodeon – and featured a strange mixture of working-class imagery (ie: *white trash*) – and fecal imaginations (ie: *poo poo*) – and homo-erotic brotherly love (ie: *boy best friends fucking*) – & baby loved to watch the show for the pure & simple pleasure that she gathered from the heavy grunting of the characters, uuhhhuhhh uuuhhhhuh uhhhhuhhh, which formed a symphony of neanderthal noises not dissimilar to the sounds that jonny t. walker iv would make, in years to come, as he fucked the living day lights out of baby.

4   baby feared pleasure most of all – for pleasure came like a tidal wave – consuming her, taking her over ... *pl-pl-pl-llppppl-pleasure* – *pl-=pleasss- pleasssure* ... she could hardly imagine herself without a crutch & a cane & a steel cannon ball tethered to her ankle; it just seemed so natural to assume the position of gimp. she felt like a cripple in a dunce cap, stomping around w. out her cane, swinging her gnarly nub of leg with glee in the open streets. what else would she do, what else would she be, what else would she become? she smiled, a bright smile – one lone black tooth winked.

5   what would language become if not sedated by psychiatry? what grammar broken, what verbs torn? what syntax hung out on the parched dry plain? it seemed so very sensible, so very obvious. psychiatry would root out the impurities within language and within those who receive language, and it would begin, of course, with the writers of language. it would begin, of course, with baby.

b/c mother didn't like to intrude, but there mother was:
mother! flipping! lights!

whut r u doin up @ this hour babbbbeeeee

im eating dog food[6]

oh / [pause.] *can i have sum?*

baby didn't know what to say, baby didn't know what to do.
she didn't want to give mother her dog food
b/c dog food was baby's food & baby didn't want to give up
      baby food: *uhhhhhhhhhhhhhhhhhhhhhhh*

... mmmmmmm ... baby glanced back & forth, back & forth...

wwwwwweeeellllllllllll ... leeeemmmmmeeeeeee seeeeee...

---

6   baby came into doctor goodall's office one day swimming in fear. she was convinced that she was rotten, detestable. she was convinced
    she was detestable for creating a world where babies raped babies & babies ate babies & dog food seemed the more nutritious choice
    than the salad bar at Whole Foods. *what should i do??* baby cried out. [*pause. gulp. wait awhile.*] doctor goodall crossed her legs,
    tapped on her pen, and gave a small smile. she knew the perfect elixir. she knew the perfect elixir to fix baby's madness, to strap
    down her ferocious mind – the mind that controlled the tongue, the tongue which spoke the words that should never, ever be spoken.
    psychiatry would render baby perfect, it would render her stories perfect, not marked by the depravity of a baby who liked to eat
    dog food.

baby wasn't sure what to do, she wasn't sure what to say.
she didn't want to be rude, she didn't want to say no,[7]

but: she also didn't want to give up

her doggone deeeeeeeellllliiiiccccciiioooussus dog food.

[long silence. the refrigerator starts to hum.]

wwweeelllllllll ... hmmmmm ... mmmm-m-mmaaaybbbbeeeee?

[*end of scene*]

---

7 *no, i am not giving you my dog food. no, it is not yours.* No! No! No! [finger wagging "no."] [sighs, shakes head.] [drops head into
hands, one last punctuating act of desperation.] why was saying "no" always an invocation of offense? why was baby so afraid to
put her foot down and tell the world, or authority, or her mother, *no, i don't want to give you dog food. no, this is my dog food!*
was "no" really so hard? was "no" really so scary? "no." "no." "NO." "um, no." "uhhhhh... no?" [silence, lights out.] [*it was the
final "no."*]

EXECUTIVE ORDER

monday night, primetime – the finger puppets bore an array of vulgar names, although they mostly lay dormant in the grass – limp, listless as soft phalluses – *they were sleepy* – then suddenly they started prancing about in a pastoral landscape vaguely similar to Nova Scotia – a la Anne of Green Gables – but may in fact have been fabricated, the rolling green hills and blue sky constructed from plastic grass and acrylic paint – *it was the landscape, not the finger puppets, which appeared pornographic* – she would later assert. [insert a piece of logic.] [make logic a log, make logs a bridge, allow the reader to climb across.] [ah, right – *nice way to insert a metaphor.*] [logic = log] [log = bridge] [connect point a to point b.]

the finger puppets were a kind a content the state loved to mask – *and who was the state?* asked an earnest reader who didn't understand the circuitous logic of an author who had lost herself to the ravages a story that once seemed productive, fruitful – but now seemed quite simply a mess – both to the author and also the reader – *and who was the state?* the earnest reader asked again. the author looked up, she was angry, she was exhausted. she wanted to get on with a politics that seemed both circular and self-referential, she wanted to step out of the swampy muck of theory, but theory was what she knew and what she loved. theory was a house she created, though she now set it on fire. she found herself trapped. she wanted to get out, she couldn't get out. she tried to answer, she tried to move the story along.

the state regulatory board was stuffed with a bunch of skinny white feminists who loved to ring their mouths around the cock of the most powerful bull-dyke lesbian in the hall. *hmmmmm, this is it?* she murmured, she turned the pages, scanning the story. she wasn't sure, she didn't know. she didn't know if she was reading the text or writing it. she didn't know if she had entered the state legislature or the national one, but she knew the author had committed an awful offense by popping off a bunch of words that had no reason to be together, no reason to elide. she knew the author had done something wrong.

she didn't know how to depict the finger puppets in ecstasy – *while also avoiding the censorial hand of a state regulatory board* – a regulatory board which loved to come down hard on any kind of content, *content which deviated from the propaganda of the moment, which is to say, the party line.* she had waded into an area of the story which far exceeded her knowledge, far exceeded her imagination, and she refused to do research, she refused to consign herself to tedious tasks which would distinguish *artifice* from *art*, *art* from *aardvarks.* she refused what she wanted – she wanted to blow out the shell, hollow out the truth, take out the meat.

she wanted to dig her fingers in, place each story-person into her mouth, there was a little leg, there was a little hand. jenny yelped between her teeth, *don't eat me! don't eat me!* jonny t. walker iv. bellowed, *stop! stop!* as he lay helpless on her tongue. she could do nothing; the gastrointestinal process had already begun, the bile had already been released, her stomach had already begun to churn.

(*note*: the white lesbian mamas got their babies from Ethiopia & Guatemala & Korea – this was long before the leaders of those respective countries slammed down on the baby stealing economy. *sad white liberals like miss macintire, founding member of the state regulatory board, became much sadder.* [insert sad face.] oh wait, the reader is sad now, oh wait, maybe she's crying [insert a row of six plump hearts.] oh wait, there are tears now, the ink is running, a small lake is forming, letters unhinged, loosening, sliding off the page.)

(*note*: the state regulatory board was populated by a bunch of power hungry white lesbians and the author first thought they were stupid re: *scary* re: she wanted to write them off swiftly with the logic of critical race theory, but she learned quickly this would do her no good – for the white lesbians were very clever and very mean, and they strangled their adopted brown yellow babies with their own brand righteous white anti-racism that they'd learned through a host of whites-only workshops and reading groups called WWP, Wreck White Privilege, which they would later copy-write, lest their brilliant white ideas be stolen by other white people.)

baby decided *propaganda was the answer to censorship and pornography was the answer to sex* – and and and she believed this, she believed one obvious obstacle to sex would always be love – and and and baby had gone to pornography as a way to cope – *she had gone to pornography as a way to deal with the fury and madness of love* – and and and she found refuge, she found solace in bouncy tits and big rubber cocks and and and (*note:* the author used words to discover other words, she used words to discover logic, she used words to discover a logic which knew no logic, logic had been abdicated from the world she lived in – she fumbled about, she sputtered, foam on her lips, spit spooling from her mouth.)

(*note*: she lived an existence where meaning had been so abdicated from the world in which she lived, she fumbled about, she sputtered, foam on her lips – she thought meaning might be found in publication (*it was not*) – she thought meaning might be found in writing (*it was not*) – she thought meaning might be found in sex (*it was not*) – yes, there was a peculiar mix of pleasure and pain in all of those things, a peculiar mix of anticipation – then fear – then longing – and then, there was also always loss – also always, always loss – loss, a kind of loss, lost.)

GRAMSCI MEETS DOLLY AND FALLS APART

baby cringed when the super fag w. his super ego spoke into the microphone,

as if proclaiming his　　　　　*"latinidadddd"*　　　and　　　　　*"homosexualidaddd"*

canceled out his excruciatingly obvious machismo.

butttt you're reeeeallllly justttt a dommmineerrrringggg dickkkkk ...

　　　　baby had wanted to say. *dommmineeerrr-*

ringggg diccccksssss can be very, very completely gay.

latin super ego loved to talk abt　　　　　*"gramsci"*　　　& *"politics"*　　　& *"h.i.v."*

　　　　he built up gloriously intricate arguments,[1]

gleaming sky-scrapers arguments abt:　　　　*"decolonization"*　　　& *"gay butt sex"*

1　she wasn't a feminist, although she claimed to be – she wasn't radical, although she claimed to be – the words she used – "lesbian" & "feminist" & "radical" – were part of a massive cover-up that allowed her to circulate in academic circles where she could publish articles in journals and pose as an uncompromising marxist lesbian feminist, but she was really nothing of the kind. what she really wanted, at the end of the day, was a big thick dick that she could swing around and stuff in the mouths of the students she'd sometimes teach. her fantasies began and ended in patriarchy and she could imagine nothing more seductive than the dream of domination.

& "*the prison   industrial complex*"   in fast-forward   speedy construction

as if swift & quick political analysis[2]   absolved him

of the plain fact of his arrogance: it didn't, according to baby.

latin super ego was really just another queen who licked his pink & pretty lips

and smmmmmmiled for the camera   [*wink, wink*]

& received all the adulation   & all praise baby pretended   to abhor.

he'd wear his tiara & curtsy as he strut the catwalk in silver stilettos, candy-colored:
confetti   blooming & bursting waving   and grinning

and   sashhhhaying his hips down the walk ...

---

2 baby had drinks w. a senior male colleague, who baby had met a few times before. she'd thought the man impressive, which set off a tendency to ramble and bloviate and generally make a fool. they met at a local mexican joint one evening and baby couldn't help but snarl at "those stupid smelly waiters" – most especially "the one wearing an ugly sombrero." her colleague studied decolonization, Aztlán. it took him a few minutes to get his bearings, then interject and when he did, it got heated. he rolled out a long, mean diatribe where he threatened to fire baby, extinguish her grants, and place her in the ghetto of the university's most notorious infidels, The Office of Academic Accountability, ie University Jail.

are we at a labor & feminism conference?!?

    is this a critical ethnic studies symposium?!? baby thought

... or are we on the catwalk at commes des garçons?!?!?!?

baby couldn't tell.   it all seemed so confusing,

the way people trumpeted   their identities   like fashion statements

flipping from one   to the next   to the next

a rotating wardrobe of empty jargon   each term out-trending the next

    mixing &   matching   *queer & poly*   *& womxn*   *& fag*

& wom-man   *& womyn*   *& cis*   *& -siiiis*   *& ssii- cisss*

... she couldn't keep track;   she couldn't keep track of the styles   the fads   the colors

    the shapes, the sizes   she couldn't keep track of any of it[3] ...

---

3 baby needed more lesbians, she needed a community of lesbians, she needed lesbians, but she didn't know if she was a lesbian, on top of it all. she'd deduced, at last, that her lesbianism was really a reaction to hating men, instead of truly loving women – *she didn't love anyone, she only hated herself* – she didn't know, was this enough to be a lesbian? baby didn't know – then there was also the small thing that she'd fucked a guy six months ago, tasted his dick in her mouth – it was a small thing, except it wasn't – she had been horribly lonely, it had been years since anyone had touched her. she spent one night with this man and then pursued him with a kind of bottomless desperation that only the hopeless can know. he'd filed a restraining order and she ended up thinking, *well, maybe i'd be better if i was gay* –

... she wanted to be *hip* & *cool* & *oh-so-rrraaadddiiccaaall*,

but she didn't know what to do: she didn't know what to say:

didn't you need all that stuuuuuuff? didn't you need all that stufffffffff

to be really down for the cause?[4] oh my oh my oh my ... baby needed to go shopping;

she needed to look cuuuuuute.   she didn't need to craft her argument;

she didn't need to sharpen her rhetorical skills;[5]

she needed to look right for the part...

the labor & feminism conference opened on friday @ 7 PM & ended monday @ 8 PM

... & the keynote began @ 6 PM w/ mister latin super ego slated

to give the golden address –

---

4 this was academia, there was no community, there were only corporations: *corporations of gays, corporations of radicals, corporations of queers.*

5 the terms "gay" & "lesbian" & "radical" hadn't erased her lonely ticks, hadn't undone her glacial sadness. she still scratched her crotch alone in the bathroom, she still hoarded boxes of feral cats. sometimes baby would rub up against the corner of a couch or a table, feel its pointed corner, hope it might offer some sort of edge through which pleasure might enter. it did for a moment. then she remembered her loneliness and went to the kitchen to heat up macaroni and cheese.

oh, oh, oh!   *yes, yes, yes!*   mister latin super ego[6]   w. his GRADE-A

tenure-track job   & fancy publisher   & conference talks galore –

– *yes, yes, yes!*   mister latin super ego was the keynote speaker at a conference

baby had long been eager to attend & colonize & dominate ...

& though she was never close to being cast as the "keynote speaker"

baby did manage to sneak herself into a panel

that would happen on sunday at 3 PM

          in a damp cob-webbed basement with a handful of pimply & pasty

academic-wanna-be-types who fumed at their lowly status inside the castle –

even after they'd published sparkling peer-reviewed papers!

even after they'd completed 5,000,000,000 words of their dissertations!

even after they'd taken out boat-loads of loans to complete their PHD!

---

6   baby hated queers because they reminded her of a freedom she had yet to discover, queers reminded her of joy that she couldn't yet allow herself – yet she herself was a total dyke and lesbianism seemed to provide her w. some sort of protection from the scourge of patriarchy – *which it didn't, because it couldn't* – and baby found herself, often, time and time again, in loveless relationships w. fat butch girls and wondering when all the fun would begin.

this is was the prize?

this is was the prize? an audience of 3 sad

looking white boys

crouched in the basement for some godforsaken panel...

re-peat! re-verse! re-hearse!

  & the story of baby is this:
    & the story of baby is this: & the story of baby is this:

baby has been living on the streets for 1 year & 2.3 months & 4 days.

she's got a backpack (north-face) which holds her entire livelihood:
1 toothbrush
1 toothpaste tube (tom's of maine)
4 sweatshirts
3 pairs of socks
2 jeans (diesel)
2 pj bottoms
1 tank
all her money (38 dollars, which comes in the form of a few crumpled 1 dollar bills
 & hundreds of round sacagawea coins
which land in her coffee cup, which she uses to shake & rattle
 & ask for money$ ...)

most days, she sits on the corner of 4th & main - whispering into her cup,
humming a song,
 gossiping w. sacagawea,
playing her harmonica & snapping some tunes
 w. chickadees & chipmunks & grasshoppers
& other street-dwellers who are more than just scenery
 but who've become baby's friends.

one day,
baby meets a girl named jenny lowenberg –
and the two strike up a conversation & w. in minutes baby captivates jenny
        w. the long & tragic story of how she ended up crunched up on the corner of main
sleeping on a cardboard box, rattling a coffee cup
        & smiling w. 3 very rotten teeth in her front mouth.

geeeeeeee gollllleeeee says jenny

& before long jenny has whipped up a story,
        gathered bits of bramble & wood
& built a store-front charity – aka money collection campaign –
        w. pieces of baby's story...

& *poooooooooofffff*

there she goes – baby is made & remade: baby becomes a "charity case"
                a piece of social justice propaganda, a sexy homeless gal w. a sexy story
a toothless bitch who somehow seemed less bitchy & witchy,
                although remained very clearly & very really, toothless.

baby often heard jenny lowenberg tell her story,
        & the story sounded like a technicolor nightmare of a lifetime movie,
replete w. gene wilder as the evil stepfather (*aka willy wonka*)
                in a top hat & sporting a dapper wooden cane.

        "baby was 16 when ..."

"drugs & crack & an abusive bipolar stepfather"
... "no, no, crack not coke" ... "no, no" ... "crack"
... "yes, yes" ... "bipolar w/o lithium" ... "rapid
cycling" ... "began when she was 10 & stopped
when she was" ... "homeless" ... "yes." ... "jingle,
jingle, jingle" ... "salvation army" ... "no, not the
creepy santa clause" ... "really sad" ... "please give
your support" ...

jenny loved to talk abt baby & all the suffering baby bore. she never talked of her own (suffering) because baby's seemed so goddamn spectacular and jenny's (suffering) seemed quite drab by comparison. *Bipolar! Homeless! Lesbian!* it all seemed so fun, it all seemed so fucked & jenny could not get enough. such an insatiable appetite jenny had for baby – for consuming baby – *Chomp! Chomp! Chomp! – Finger-lickin Good!* – that she swore she'd become positively swollen w. suffering ...

... but: it was not suffering jenny consumed, but *spectacle*

& spectacle had its origins in ... *POWWW !!! KAAA-POPPP !!! KAZZZAAAM!!!*
         ... & every corporate advertising wing
                  of every international media conglomerate
         wh/ch told young girls what was fun & what was not
                  & who was pretty & who was not
         & what to feel & what you should *never, ever, ever feel* ...

& so jenny wrote baby's story & jenny spoke baby's story
& baby's story became "baby's story" & "baby's story" became baby's ststtttorryyy b/came
babys-- strrxxstorxxxsssssssssyyyy b/came baby's ssstsstsstttssssssss-sss-torrrrry b/cm ba----
bebeeesttttttorrreeeeeee

& what became of baby?
    & what became of baby?

XXXX THE END XXXX

[*post-script*]

& the story of baby is this
    & the story of baby is this: _____
                               (noun, adverb)

safari

on her third day in south africa, baby saw a giraffe, a rhinoceros, and a zebra having a threesome. it was her first day at the madikee game reserve in kwazulu natal, south africa, and baby didn't think she would see any animals, let alone any animals mating; she definitely didn't think she'd see three very rare animals mating with each other. yet, there they were – a giraffe, a rhinoceros, and a zebra each pounding each other in a mad, tropical blur, each exploding like tiny bright fireworks.

back in scarsdale, baby had a whole crew of creatures in the corner of her bedroom: a snake named harpsichord which she usually called harpy, a jackrabbit named louis, and two fat hamsters named tweetle-dee and tweetle-dum who were brothers and lolled about indolently. baby had saved twelve jelly jars of quarters to make this trip[1] and it was very exciting, then, that she was now in kwazulu natal among wild animals, not pet animals.

while baby watched, a little man peddled up to baby with an ice-cream cart[2] that had, splayed across the belly, the words "umlungu." she gave him a nod, transfixed by the animals. she did not know but "umlungu" meant "white person" and here, in south africa, baby too was a "umlungu."[3]

she ordered a strawberry ice cream cone – "rainbow sprinkles, too, please," – and the little man fussed behind the cart. when he appeared with her cone, she gave him one rand note and swiftly returned her gaze to the animals humping on the horizon.

---

1 mother and father would only let her go if she made an estimated one-fourth financial contribution to the trip because mother and father were goddamn sure that their little baby was not going to be a spoiled little mother-fucking baby.

2 there were a great many carts that speckled the horizon; carts that sold tee-shirts, bottled water, keychains, and dinky bobble-head dolls of zulu warriors. those dolls, baby knew, were racist. those dolls baby surely did not buy.

3 yes, baby was white, even though father was a second-generation ashkenazi jew and mother, who was of german ancestry and whose ancestors settled in the minnesota in the eighteenth century, volunteered with urban youth at the ymca and liked to wear dashikis in july.

"yum, yum" said baby and settled into her collapsible chair.

suddenly a leopard sauntered over; its pink tongue slipped out like a wet secret and began to lick baby's ice-cream cone. usually, she was fussy about her food,[4] but she waited patiently as the leopard took his time licking the ice-cream.

"you like that?" asked baby.

the leopard continued to lick, not saying a word.

"aw, you do – you do like that," said baby and gave a smile. again, there was quiet but for the licks of the leopard.

a few indian business men drove by and ordered two ice cream cones as well. the truck was rimmed with five armed guards and when a herd of zebras appeared, the men dropped their cones and whipped out their cameras.

they click-click-clicked as the zebras stampeded away, the red african dust covering their business suits.

the leopard sniffed the fallen ice cream and nuzzled the cones, and then returned to lick baby's ice cream.

the leopard smiled and baby smiled back. the leopard licked, and licked again.

---

4 baby brought with her four jumbo tubs of smooth jiffy peanut butter in the very likely event that she didn't like the native food. what she did find herself liking, however, were braii boerewors because they reminded her of hot dogs.

"may i call you nelson mandela?" baby asked.

the leopard leapt up and devoured the entire ice cream cone in one gulp. baby began to cry and then the leopard leapt up and ate baby too.

chapter one, the great white fear

baby has fallen in love with a big black boy w. an enormous dick
                                                           &

        mother & father are godawfully angry.

did he hafta be black baby?? did he hafta be black??

        they shout across the dinner table.

his name is snoop (dogg) and he's got t-t-thffreee gold caps in the back of his mouth and one in the front. he'd like to get a fourteen karat cap, preferably w. a tiny diamond stud in the center – but he can't afford it right now. it costs 300 bucks and his bank account reads 12. what else does snoop got? he's got a killer smile – he brushes thrice daily, flosses once – and he's got a whole long list of dream-jobs that he rattles off in his head: ganja-grower, ganja-smokah, ganja dealer, president of the l.g.a., the legalize ganja association, which is headquartered on the island of jamaica, a short walk from a turquoise sea that ruffles to the white sandy beach where snoop would sit with a fat blunt in his mouth and a harem of women gyrating next to him. damnnnn, dis is da life, snoop thinks, sipping his margarita and exhaling a long plume of smoke.

papa, you'll love him, baby implores.

        he's kind & gentle & he loves me

as·no man has ever loved me. just wait

        til you meet him: he's coming for dinner on thursday.

father shoots a fiery glance at mother, clearly quite distressed. father is a litigator @ the law firm of shreve, crump & low and his clients consist of large multinationals w. a focus on businesses in oil rich countries like kuwait & dubai. he believes in equality & freedom for all, but not for young baby – father cannot bear the thought of black dick in wet, white pussy. it's too much, it's just too much.

father & mother & baby live at the end of a cul-de-sac in the great town of maplewood, land of the uuuunited states. they love maplewood, they love the house they live inside: the green grass, white picket fence, the big front porch and bertha – they love bertha. bertha came to live w. mother & father & baby when baby was just a wee thing – she was just a knot of pink flesh asleep in the crib.

altho that was years ago b/f baby was grown b/f baby knew boys b/f baby knew black boys

& now mother sighs & whistles for bertha: *bertha darling, bertha come here –*

we need a bit of wine.

  will you get us wine?

secretly mother likes snoop & she's secretly scandalized by baby's choice of paramour. mother doesn't know many black men, but she always found those she knew particularly comely. there was howard taft, the podiatrist who worked at the corner mall and played golf with father; there was andrew jackson, who lived on maplewood and traded commodities; and occasionally she'd exchange pleasantries with ulysses s. grant, who worked at the gas station up near the high school and always shaved a few dollars off mother's repair work.

she didn't know ulysses well, though once, mother saw him picking up the newspaper in his undies early one blue morning. much to her surprise, the sight gave mother a volcanic eruption of ecstasy which culminated in her singing puccini's aria *"htoislkmh oijlkdf"* at the top of her lungs and then shivering in the bathroom where she had been peeping from the window.

father lay asleep in bed, unable to get mother horny the previous night: he had tried her vibrator, he tried his porn.

he had tried his quick & agile tongue, so eager he was to offer cunnilingus to his woman, slow or fast or wet or buttery or however she might have wanted. none had worked; nothing could turn mother on as black men could turn mother on.

mother had also liked to catch glimpses of the black basketball players on television, mother always found those men so-very becuuummming. she liked how they'd swarm on the court, making big dark heaving hives; she liked to catch sight of their colorful boxers, their head-bands, their hard, flat stomachs and the trail of black curls that lead down to their [*expletive*]. but mother couldn't say such things, certainly not to father. father would be inflamed, surely he would - the thought of mother's fantasy life made him livid with envy.

and yet:
on thursday, in three days and five-plus hours,
        mother's fantasy life will walk through the door.

she keeps her mouth closed, purses her lips
        & swishes her wine.

then she shouts:

bertha!!! bertha!!! where are you???

bertha arrives, her pin-a-fore a black & white doily.
    she pours mother's wine.

i don't know, baby. father says, shaking his head.
    you've done some wild things in the past, but this: this is beyond mention.

this: this takes the cake. this is inconceivable.

the problem is he's black, daddy?
    it's inconceivable that he's black? asks baby.

father falls silent.
    well, yes.

father dabs his napkin in lemon water
    & pats his face.

we'll have to wait until thursday, says mother.
    thursday young snoop dogg arrives.

"lilacs, lavender, and other mysteries"

baby didn't know exactly when she started to hate rich white people,
        but it began sometime between 6 and 8 o'clock.

[6:15 PM, RITZ] missus baroness, the beautiful baroness mother
        of jonny t. walker iv. walked into The Ritz Carlton

to meet our dear baby. (note: baby had recently been fired from
        her job @ Rite-Aid & she had dentist bills to pay

and Adderall to pop and a tummy desperately in need of stapling
        & so – she was feeling a wee bit anxious.)

since baby was down & out on casss$h, she'd come to ask missus baroness
        if she might be a Maid or Nanny or Butler

on the walker estate. (note: missus baroness wanted to meet baby at The Ritz
        not because she would dine with her; heccccccck no

she brought her to The Ritz because she thought that if she showed baby
        her own decadent world and then flipppppppped her middle finger at baby

– *no, you don't belong. no, this is not yours* – then baby might better understand
        what kind of world she'd be expected to serve, but certainly never inhabit.)

[6:49 PM, RITZ] missus baroness and baby sat on a couch in the lobby
      & baby dipped her head & said yesssssssm'am yesssssssm'am to

missus baroness' musings, which were:

1. ritz is gooooorgeous at night.

2. do you think those are lilacs?

3. oh no, they must be lavender.

4. i don't have a green thumb, at alllllll.
      (note: missus baroness was preemptively self-deprecating –
                              as all good rich ladies should be.)

5. i spend far too much time in the sun, as it is.

6. why lets talk, baby, lets talk.

baby was first enthralled with missus baroness, her creamy white skin
& her sweet, cotton-candy voice. her eyes went goooooogly (at her beauty)
& her stomach went goooooopy (at her richness).

baby felt she could not say much, so overwhelmed was she
that didn't know what to say, she didn't know what to do.
she felt a knot tighten in her belly and she croaked out some words:

w-wh-w-h-wwwh-wwhutt-ttt-t-t-ttt
        wwwwh-whut-t-t-t-t-t do you want me to do ??

missus baroness sighed, as if baby had said the loveliest thing,
        as if baby had given her a bouquet of fresh-picked roses
and not the mangled thorns of language, which was all baby could muster.

missus baroness smiled and looked into baby's eyes: what a wonderful question;
        what a dear little baby.

[7:04 PM, RITZ] as missus baroness talked more, baby became more fearful
        & also more furious.

yyyikkkkkkkeeeessssssssssssss & *eeeeeeeeeeeeekkkkk* & also *uuuuuggggggggggghhhhh*

        were some sounds that cycled through baby's mind; though she grinned
& giggled & spread her legs wide, wide, wide ...

... & the nicer missus baroness was, the more baby doubted her.

missus baroness asked baby all sorts of questions, peering into her life,
        as if she could pull back the dark curtain with a sprinkling of pleasantries.

she presumed a kindness, an intimacy *sccooffffffffff!*   that baby just couldn't bear.

she couldn't bear how whhhhhite missus baroness was and also how nice.

it just didn't quite square, it just didn't quite match. (*a + b did not*, she thought, *equal c*.)
(*rich + white could not*, she thought, *equal nice. it just couldn't. it couldn't.*)

> we'll be friends, missus baroness said & gave baby a wink.
> we'll be friends, darling.

> the best work comes out of near, dear friendship, i think. don't you?

what does this woman waaaaant? baby kept thinking. *what's up her sleeve?*

she imagined two devil horns hidden beneath the crop of white hair, perfectly coiffed to hide her demon-ics & plate-tectonics. she imagined her heart & lungs & blood pumping black tar, visions of lucifer leapt as missus baroness prattled on. (note: missus baroness was not at all hip to the homoerotic underpinnings of her prattling and her hetero-normative fist, nor was she aware that dear little baby for whom she'd coo and she'd moo found these remarks mostly quite degrading, although sometimes – yes: sometimes, baby found them a teensy bit hot.)

[7:55 PM, RITZ] baby smiled & giggled & sucked in her stomach.
    & mother walker continued to blather ...

blllllllllllaaah blahhhhhhhhh *yes, yes! it's perfect! we're perfect!* blllllllahhhhh blaaaaahhhh blahhhhh blahhhhhh *o! o! o! i don't know! i don't know why we're so perfect!* blahhhhh blahhhhhh

blahh *yes! yes! we're shimmering!* blahhhhhh blaaaaahhhhh *yes! yes! we're gold!* blllllahhhhh

blahhhh blahhhhh *o! o! o! yes! perhaps! we're not gold! we're pink! we're pink gold!* blahhh blahh

blahhh blahhhhh *pink gold! pink gold! pink!* blahhhhhhh blahhhhhhhh blahhhhhhhh

mother continued to talk as baby drifted off into FantasyLand,
she thought about what it would be like to be a Maid or a Nanny or Butler

on the walker estate, she thought about what it might be like to be a walker herself
– BABY WALKER – though jonny t. had refused her demands for marriage & love

& fidelity, she still hoped that he might, perhaps, submit to her sexual overtures,
though he did say *get away from me you freeeeeeeaaakkkk*

the last time she offered
to give him a blow job...

baby still hoped, though, by being the Maid or Nanny or Butler
she might parlay the position in some sort of wife-y or trophy-like gig

where she could sit on jonny t.'s lap & show him her butt & lick his 6 fingers *alllllllllllllllllllllllll   niiiiiiiiighhhhhhht   looooooooooong*

baby thought of all this, as mother walker yammered away ...
bllllah blaaaah blaaaah-ing
       & chit-chit-chat-ing

& tee-hee-eeeing all to baby's very raw ears. (they bled, in fact.)
& then, at last, mother walker asked the golden question:

do you want the job?

CELEBRITY SMACK DOWN! warhol versus grace of monaco

SUPERMODELS * GET * FAT * AND * MALNOURISHED * SOMALIAN * CHILDREN * ARE *PLACED * ON * THE * CATWALK * AT * COMMES * DES * GARÇONS * ADOLF * HITLER * AND * OPRAH * WINFREY * SIT * DOWN * FOR * THANKSGIVING * DINNER * AND * DISCUSS * THEIR * COMMON * ANCESTRY * HIJAB-WEARING * SAUDI * TEENAGER * IS * SECRET * BULIMIC * BUT * REVEALS * HER * STORY * TO * THE * WORLD * "YOU ARE NOT ALONE," * SHE * SAYS * RICHARD * GERE * FINDS * A * MOUSE * STUCK * UP * HIS * ASS * AMIDST * UPROAR * FROM * VEGAN * ACTIVISTS * JENNY * LOWENBERG * DISCOVERS * SHE * IS * ACTUALLY * ½ * BLACK * AND * TAKES * UP * THE * NIGGERIZING * NAME * J.LO * JOHNNY * T * WALKER * IV * SEX * TAPES * REVEAL * HE * DRESSES * UP * AS * THOMAS * JEFFERSON * AND * FUCKS * BLACK * SLAVE * GIRLS * UP * THE * ASS * THE * ONE * CALLED * SALLY * HEMMINGS * LOOKS * LIKE * A * LIGHT * SKINNED * VERSION * OF * DAVIDA * DAVIDSON * NOW * THERE * YOU * GO * STAR * LIGHT * STAR * BRIGHT * SHINE * BRIGHT * SHINE * BRIGHT * MIDNIGHT * TONIGHT *

baby loved the idea that she could be a huge empty symbol, her face flattened on the side of a bus or train or high in the sky splayed on a blimp's big bloated belly. baby was an artist, what could she say? she longed for fame! she longed for acclaim! what was private or personal she liked only in so far as she could package & sell it in the gift shops of MOCA or LACMA or on the mean streets of gallery row. her private life existed only for the consumption of hungry art-herds & hungry art-fans; she had shaken hands with the devil & sold her soul to large art-institutions & art-executive-boards, & by god – *baby was going to ca$h in!* she was going to make a buck off her art, just as she'd made a buck off her lily white skin.

art was the same thing, baby realized, as everything else. art was a popularity contest which baby was always going to lose, unless she threw in her cards, put on some lipstick, and sucked vigorously on the dick of the most popular art person in the room. art was political, just as her body was political. art operated much like the hallowed halls of congress, with a handshake & a wink & ten million dollars in the pockets of halliburton.

art was: art was: art was executive search committees & corporate backers & facilities maintenance & candy-land corruption & mile-long elevators & museums shaped like mollusks & ill-prepared tour guides & shit framed in gold ... all this was to say that baby knew art was not-art – *art was politics, politics was power* – art was pre-spect-ive & *art was the speculative pre-spect-ive of collective capital.* art was really just something some knuckleheads decided to call art. art was: art was collective & art was capital & art was bogus & baby was bogus ...

baby, of course, feared that she'd be rejected from art-institutions & art-people & arty-art; sure, she'd sold out, she'd rejected her *true self*, so she might become *a bigger self.* she'd hoped to become, in the process of selling, more clearly an arty-artist – or an artsy-artiste – or a piece of art, itself.

& so it was: the more baby sold-out, the more baby bought in: the more she craved & consumed the myth that arty art was real art & all the rest was artsy fartsy not-art ...

art matters! art doesn't matter! yee-haw!

1 - *art does matter!*

baby was sure she was better / because she thought about *mattering* & *not-mattering*
& she'd concluded it was so much better, so much more cooler / to think

art didn't matter... & she knew that art didn't matter,
but *she also performed this knowledge,*

which is to say – *she pretended that art didn't matter* [1] ...

& though baby pretended *art didn't matter*, she also pretended
she didn't matter [2] ... but behind *the patina of pretending*

that she didn't matter, she was sure *she mattered much more*
than her arty artsy artiste friends – because she knew, at least, she was better off

prostrating / at the altar of *not-mattering*
& by pretending that *she didn't matter*, she'd acquired

---

1 baby wanted to make art that was *beautiful*, she wanted to make art that reflected *the values of love and truth*, she wanted to make *art that honored the sublime*. she didn't want to be the kind of artist who made paintings that used dirty tampons & toilet paper as their primary materials, but she'd also spent her life claiming that *art didn't matter*, so what else could she make? what else could she expect?

2 baby didn't know if her modesty was simply a tactic to cover grand designs for world domination. she dreamed of *baby-art* & *baby-fame* & *baby-names* printed all over the city, all over the world. capitalism demanded that Baby Be Big! when really baby was small, and *baby was just a baby* & she didn't know what she wanted – *she couldn't know* – not within the stultifying structure of capitalism, how could she see beyond big dollar sign$ & ca$sssh...

the handsome cloak of *self-deprecation*
which was necessary for any young woman

who might be rocketed to success[3] ...

2 - art doesn't matter!

baby pitted herself against her friends[4] & she pitted herself
against art, but she did it all w. an aggressively passive exterior...

& it was all so very "self-deprecating"; it was all so very "elegant"[5] –
     the power of her illusion rested in her ability

to be a confidently self-effacing artist who showed little need
        for the accolades / she secretly coveted ...

---

3 jenny lowenberg had assumed that if she could be a sexy art waif and populate her instagram with moody images then she could somehow comport herself into a masterful artist (ie: famous artist) (ie: jenny thought fame equaled mastery). she wanted a powerful presence on social media, she didn't want to dedicate hours & hours to craft – she didn't want a facility with form, she didn't want to grapple with content. she was a sexy art waif, she had not one original thought in her head. inside her brain were enormous spreadsheets for calorie counting – *they were colorful, vibrant* – she thought nothing of art, she thought only of food and the rigor it took to be skinny.

4 baby accrued silent indictments towards her arty artsy artiste friends. *didn't they know they were making objects, not art?* didn't they know these objects should be shown in Walgreens or Best Buy, not fancy museums or empty galleries? *didn't they know that their work should be seen as commodities, not art?* they did, of course, but they didn't care. they preferred to live in the shallow illusion of their complexity and make a little ca$ssh along the way ...

5 baby wanted to make paintings where a chorus of doe eyed maidens sang melodies by the shore. she wanted to make art where cherubs picked fresh grapes from the vine. she thought beauty resided at the hollow center of Art History (re: phallic and white) – though she was wrong – *dead wrong.*

3 - art does matter but baby doesn't matter!

sigh, sigh, sigh ... *who wants faaaaame? who wants forttttttune?*
who wants their name in *us weekly* magazine?[6] (i do! i do! i do! shouted a chorus of fan-girls,
behind the ropes of the red carpet.[7]) (– *it was a natural desire* – it was, it was – baby claimed
or not-claimed – *it was natural, the need to be seen & the need to be loved ...*)

baby wanted to be seen, *really – truly seen*
she wanted to be *known*, known from *the depths of her being*,
　　　but she wasn't prepared for *what a fool it would make her* –

she wasn't prepared for *what a pathetic fool* she'd become –

... because *being seen / didn't mean* she would be *beautiful...*
it didn't mean she would be *loved*, it didn't mean she would be *known*,

it meant only that she would be *witnessed* –
　　　it meant *others would bear witness to baby* –

6　jenny lowenberg loved to talk about her creamy fantasies of painting, but she didn't know that *real art* rarely saw itself as such –
real art wasn't talked about, it was just consummated. it was made, improbably, from urgency. jenny knew no urgency, she knew no
struggle. what struggle she did know came from a botched boob job one summer; the silicon had leaked out one night and she was
rushed to the ICU after she started to stutter weird words at dinnertime. (note: she would survive to make an art installation about
the episode, where small silicon packets covered the floor of a gallery and visitors had to walk on pogo sticks to enter the space.
three visitors broke their necks on the sticks and then filed lawsuits, but daddy was a corporate lawyer and swiftly smashed them
like a bug.)

7　*the market-place was an art-space*: baby had snobby artist friends who threw parties in loft spaces. doctor goodall encouraged baby
to go to these parties, because she thought *baby needed to be a part of the marketplace*, she thought baby needed to make some
money. the truth was that the parties usually resulted in baby binge drinking or engaging in self-harm behavior, but doctor goodall
thought *baby needed to regulate her behavior, not her environment*. it was the typical thinking of a capitalist-psychologist, who
ignored the pathology of systems in favor of the individual.

4 - art doesn't matter and baby does matter!

baby's friends would come at her with "pitches"
       & "stories" & "grand opera narratives" about their "art" – why it was made,
how it was made, where it might be placed – where it might exist, when it met the world –

["museums & galleries[8] & basketball courts in bed-stuy, brooklyn –"
       once baby's arty artsy artiste friends began the foray into *totally meaningful
and tooooootally political – "social practice art"*...]

there were big thumping egos[9] behind their words, their talk of *the selfless nature of art*:
the egos thumped louder: "ME!!!!!" & "MINE!!!!!" & "LOOK AT ME!!!!!"

sure, they stood at the podium

and professed silvery words about *"the selfless nature of art"*
and *"abdicating the autonomous I"* – but all of it was, really, just a cover

for their own narcissistic concerns about fame & fortune

---

8 *the art-space was a market-place*: baby went to an art show, she wandered around, she looked at the paintings and ate a few cubes
    of cheese; then she went to the bathroom and she tore out her eyelashes. it felt good, like she'd cleared something out of her system.
    doctor goodall would later explain *female rage is often inwardly directed*, but baby didn't really care. she just wanted to find a way
    to navigate an *art-space-cum-market-place* and not be consumed by it. pulling out her eyelashes did the trick – and she appreciated
    that she could do it in the privacy of a bathroom stall.
9 *the art-space was a market-place*: there was a private showing at a gallery, and baby was invited. indeed, she felt lucky to be invited,
    she felt lucky to be apart of a world which held her hostage. the show featured work by a famous artist named johnny t. walker iv.
    and baby went to the show, as doctor goodall had encouraged. she arrived in her finest, clutching her purse. the statement tacked to
    the wall said the paintings were *scratch and sniff erotica*. there were big fuzzy vulvas in neon colors and baby scratched on the clit.
    then she ran outside, ashamed.

... & their need to make

$$$$ (they wanted money)

(& cute girls[10])

(& fashionable clothes)

(& a string of publications in *N+1* & *The Believer* & *The London Review of Books*)

... & didn't they know that *nothing mattered except baby?*

didn't they know *nothing mattered except baby-art & baby-friends & baby-fame?*

didn't they know that *only baby could be an artist* (there could only be one!) – because *only baby*

was extraordinarily & effortlessly egoless ...

5 - art does matter and baby doesn't matter!

the other side of it was, though, that baby didn't know if she really did matter –
& it was quite possible that *art did matter & baby didn't matter.*

---

10 baby could only conceive of *beauty under the aegis of capital*, she could only conceive of *aesthetics within the structure of form.* she couldn't conceive of herself beyond commodification, she couldn't conceive of her work outside of the marketplace. what was a beautiful painting if not sanctified by capital? what was a beautiful woman if not constructed by a man?

she couldn't quite wrap her head around such a proposition,

she couldn't quite understand whether *mattering*[11] might be *real*,
mattering might be *true*, mattering might *not be a joke*...

---

11 what was The Truth? what was The Answer? *did art matter or did art not-matter?* baby didn't realize that *art did matter*, but it
didn't matter in the ways that she thought it mattered. it wasn't an audience or a market that made art matter, though art might
have some – or *none!* – of those things. *art mattered because it changed people.* that was it! that was the end of the story! that was
the end of the proof!

The Diagnostic and Statistical Manual of White People

white-guys come in all sorts of breeds:

1) *hyper=aggressive* + *over-assertive*, whose mother never loved him
       & fears he has a tiny dick & overcompensates
by bludgeoning the feminine spirits of estrogen & aphrodite + playing videogames
       & drinking 18 litres of beer a night & hhhhhufffffffinggg
& pufffffffingggg & hullllkkkking his steroid-addled body
       thru high-school & pretending to be a pea-brained retard – when in fact he's not!
(he's not?) – he knows the answer to the question: "Teacher, Toni Morrison
       Is the Author of The Bluest Eye, Written in 1984, Copyright Random House."
2) *slicky self-congratulatory righteous rocker,* who plays reggae
       & loves jazz & just recently got (over)educated on topics
of racism & discrimination & colonization – by reading
       Howard Zinn, of course – & w. shocking alacrity
jumped on the bandwagon of anti-racism-sexism-facism-ablism
       & now proclaims "White Male Privilege" to his Trinidadian nanny
who looks @ him cross-eyed when he tries to talk
       abt The Feminization of Labor & The Horrors of Colonization
& says: "as a person of austro-hungarian ancestry – who occupies
       a place @ the apex of this enormous country + who holds a Y chromosome
& enormous wads of ca$$$$h i want to say: IM SORRY. TELL ME
       IM NOT A BAD WHITE PERSON. IM A GOOD WHITE PERSON."

3) *artsy euro squatter*, who subsists off great big bricks of ca$$$h from
        Germany or other neo-socialist countries
that support artists: "And Thus The Nation"
        the artsy euros brush their (nappy??) hair 3 times per year; & live in squalid
splendor & make big loping abstract paintings (side note: vacuous)
        & keep their feelings - rocket-tight - bottled(tite) – nitrite-tight
in a Fanta can – *fizzzzzeeeeeeeeeeeeeeeee* – only 2 explode @ mention of:
  a) hitler
  b) the holocaust
  c) inmigración 2 dresden, esp.

the murder
      of the pregnant   muslim   woman
Marwa el-Sherbini
      who was stabbed
          to death: in the courtroom
that wednesday   *July 1, 2009*
      on schloßplatz 1   01067   R I P

There Is No God   *But God*
     And Germans Are The Enemy of God.

dear wartime, dear bird

she yip yips
    did you get enough protein
    did you wash the dishes
    did you do your taxes
    did you go to the doctor
    did you get your teeth cleaned
    did you go wash the car
    did you brush your teeth
    did you put on deodorant
    did you take your vitamins
    did you smile like i said to smile
    did you talk like i said to talk (*please and thank you, please and thank you*)
    did you wash your pits when you showered
    did you use antibacterial soap when you washed your pits
        (*not regular soap you know that's no good now don't you*)
    did you use the proper pronoun when you wrote the thank you note
    did you write the right thank you note
    did you write the thank you note
    did you smile
    did you smile and say thank you
    why didn't you smile
    did you get the blood test
    did the blood test go okay
    did you smile

did you smile
       did you smile like i said to smile
did you smile
did you smile

sssemeopoemesss

AS A SIMULACRA:

baby's *Art-Self* & baby's *Self-Self* confused her
     & she found herself

so consumed by being an artist
     & all its attendant demands – psychotherapy

appointments, glamorously tattered denim, suicidal
     tendencies – and she'd lost track of the daily

pleasures of living that had nothing to do w. art, nothing
     to do w. *The Violent Project of Documentation*[1]

(e.g.: strolling through the park
     at nine a.m. & watching the old ladies practice

tai chi; steaming milk for her coffee & forgoing
     the tabernacle of starbucks, eyes

---

1 the year baby took art classes at the local YMCA she threw approximately 18 hissy fits; her mother witnessed each one with increasing exasperation. baby would throw her watercolors on the carpet & scream, *im an artttissstteeee! im an artttttisteeee!* sometimes, she'd break a canvas, other times, she'd destroy her beloved dioramas. she'd roll on the carpet, covered in blotches of watercolor paints, toss her fists in the air and fight for something she could neither name nor fully understand. what she was fighting for, really, was her *humanity* – which had never been afforded her – *not really* – in the first place, but which she'd discovered through a series of art classes that transpired over the course of one autumn in the basement of a nearby YMCA.

hungry for nothing, *Hungry for Emptiness,*
     The Wide Expanse of Experience –

Not L-A-N-G-U-A-G-E Pinned Down and Stuck
     To a Page.) there was little art

in her relentless search for art,[2]
     baby would often complain.

baby had broken down in a fit
     of tears[3] – proclaiming *the emmmmptiness of it alllll*

the emmmmptiness of it alllll & proclaiming her very, really, truly sincere desire

     for *mmmmeaning & aaaaauthenticity –*

from which only rrrrreal art could be made.

---

2 baby's art projects included projecting a series of tabloid headlines onto the wall, constructing a tiny pre-civil war diorama, and building a bridge of pixie stix that stretched the length of a city block. she called each piece – respectively – serious art project no. 1, no. 2, no. 3, etc etc – because *everything was art and everything was serious, god damn it!* baby believed this from the core of her being – even when her classmates would laugh at her, as they did when she'd flailed about in a tub full of mayonnaise (serious art project no. 7) and even when they'd stuck lead pencils up her nose (serious art project no. 12) and even when they'd nearly choked her to death with a collar made for dogs (serious art project no. 16).

3 critique had become an opportunity for baby to dominate through an intellectual arrogance which mushroomed along with a growing vocabulary. baby kept a running list of obnoxious art terms in the back of her notebook, which included words like "indeterminacy" and "paraliterary" and while she had no idea what these words meant, they sounded fun and she loved saying them. baby's classmates would suck their breath whenever "paraliterary" popped out, and they'd stand listlessly, uttering "ummmm" and "ahhhhh" – before baby unleashed a torrent of garbled art-crit garbage.

could there be art in farts? / art in pop-tarts
      & candy hearts? / could there be art[4]

failed art? / art in baby's bald need for art?
      art! / art! / art! / baby wished there was art![5]

in everything, but mostly there was not.
      ... the truth was life was hard & boring

& often disappointing & tearing it down
      "for the sake of art" was really a vain attempt

to reconcile w. an unhappy existence
      which offered little beauty & little redemption.

& yet: & yet: she pined & she tore & she made
      SERIOUS ART PROJECT no. 1, & no. 2, & no. 3,

---

4 the art program at the YMCA was run by a feeble but well-meaning man named mister bouchard who liked yogurt & knitting & considered art a craftsman tradition that ended in nineteenth-century impressionism. baby would inject the classes with the heady conceptualism she'd gathered from the pompous art critics she'd come to love; she'd bark questions at her classmates, referencing dada & duchamp & the failures of representation in a loud, angry voice that mister bouchard would tentatively ask baby to lower. *why are you trying to silence me?* she'd snarl back. *why are you such a chauvinist pig?*

5 baby's most precious hour each week was spent in the office of doctor goodall, where she recounted the minute details of her daily struggles. most of these struggles revolved around existential loneliness & fluctuations of weight & the typical complaints of a spoiled child. doctor goodall raked in a solid $550 per hour to witness the bottomless needs of spoiled children, such as baby, and she often whipped up a diagnosis or two in the space of one short session. Cried at Titanic? *Severe Clinical Depression!* Misplaced your keys? *Attention Deficit Disorder!* Teacher hugged you funny? *Childhood Sexual Abuse!* each new diagnosis gave doctor goodall more hours & thus more cash – the clean logic of supply & demand firmly at work. baby didn't realize any of this, of course, but the diagnoses piled on high. baby's mother believed artistry was built upon each mental quirk, each pathological twitch – *bipolar type II & panic disorder with rapid cycling anxiety & infrequent acute depression* – each diagnosis gave baby yet another chance to execute another serious art project no. ...

& no. 4, & no. 5, & no. 6, & no. 7 ... & these projects gave
her meaning ... these projects gave her life.

... & so she took out her pens, she picked up her crayons,
she cleaned up her mess, & she began to draw.

SEVEN STEPS TO A GNARLY AWAKENING

STEP 1 – "the meaning of life" – and its corollary, *fulfillment* – was an equation
      baby was constantly, secretly trying to solve.

how could "the meaning of life" include such superficial bitches
      like jenny & davida & lila? how could "the meaning of life" be hung
on the glittering ladder of *power & privilege*?

did power give things meaning? did meaning exist beyond –
      all that silliness, all those surfaces, all those plastics?
baby didn't know, she didn't know.

was it *happiness*? did happiness = *achievement*? did achievement = success + love?
      or did *meaning* = joy + suffering with a sprinkle of *happiness*?
she didn't know. she honestly didn't know.

baby thought that surely, surely – meaning had to include
      the variables of *truth* + *love* + *power* ; but did *meaning* = fulfillment?
if *meaning* = fulfillment then why did she pine after popularity

like a dog w. its blue tongue / dragging to the floor?
      … & so "the meaning of life" equaled, baby surmised – exhausted
w. thinking & scribbling & shuffling the cards –

"the meaning of life" – she decided, finally, at last – once and for all,
       equaled *popularity* + *social hierarchy* + *friends*

      & baby's friends were pretty, rich things –

STEP 93 – baby hadn't heard of terms like "unreliable narrator" and "post-modern apothecary." she didn't understand such terms & quite honestly, she didn't care for them. she didn't care for universities or professor-goats or any of the verbose motherfuckers who liked to pontificate about literary theory.

    she wanted to write!
she wanted to write! unimpeded by the barrage of w-o-r-d-s
    that wouldn't stop –
w-o-r-d-s   that would pour over her / like clear evian water.

(note: there had been a food fight in the cafeteria & jenny lowenberg had "accidentally" thrown a bowl of red pasta sauce on baby's head, and then kindly took baby to the bathroom where she poured evian water on baby's hair – as if to clean it, as if she cared.)

STEP 4 – what didn't make sense, baby knew, was how desperately she searched for silence within words. she hated words & yet she needed them. she hated language & yet she used it. this was all she seemed to be able to say ...

$$1 - 2 - 3 \quad \& \quad A - B - C$$

it was the same repetitive loop on the record player; it was the same spin-cycle
in the dishwasher: sense & non-sense, sense & non-sense ...
        ... sense & non-sense ... *wake up, you dumb bourgeois bitch!*
bertha had wanted to say, *sense is real – you make sense – it makes sense –*
    – cents – sense – scent(s) ...

baby wasn't ready to believe she made sense;
baby wasn't ready to believe in cents.
baby would continue to write pallid poems & scratch the surface of reality
and press the same hopeless key of the TI-83 calculator over & over & over again ...

this is it! this is it! this is it!

$$x + z = ABC \quad x + BBB = CC$$
$$x + z = ABC \quad x + BBB = CC$$
$$x + z = ABC \quad x + BBB = CC$$

STEP 23 – bertha knew baby better than baby knew herself ... *but baby was still convinced that the way to know oneself was through oneself,* and so she continued to fall into the same solipsistic traps that led her to the self-help section of barnes & noble where she'd pick up a few gems, like eckhart tolle and doctor phil, and prayed to god that these woke white men could help her recover from her depression and crippling anxiety.

STEP 12 – baby didn't trust herself at all, not ever, not a lick.
she trusts herself only when confronted with the awful reality that she herself is all
she can trust: the truth is baby's the last stop on the block,
she's the only real statue to which she can pray.

      sure, there is the statue of liberty, the green mildew goddess
whose skirts lap at the island nation of man-hattan, the greatest borough on earth,
      a city that teems with promise of eight dollar cappuccinos & polish tea crackers
         & a faux down-market hipster aspirational flavor.

      ... sure, there is liberty, there are hipsters, there is doctor phil.
      ... sure, baby could find *hope* – or – maybe *direction* – or maybe
the slim compass needle set clearly on *meaning* & *community* ...
      ... but really, truly, baby would always find herself –
a self placed on a *shelf* – a baby doll – a: an empty – cracked – *baby-doll*

      if only baby realized this, bertha thought. *if only baby knew ...*

STEP 445 – what bertha knew and what bertha wrote ...
1. baby is post-suicidal.
2. baby is "neutral as yogurt."
3. baby is loved.
4. baby is loved.
5. baby is loved.

amour de golden arches

she wakes at 5 a.m. & heats her curlers in their plastic nest
she arranges & rearranges her perfumes

au de lampsxxx   chanel no. 6   sam-i-am

she pauses for a moment,   considers the weather,   considers her dress
considers the boys she might want   to canoodle ...

        then goes the spider-wand,
the runaway   tube of lipstick,
the alchemical whimsy   of powder-puffs! she loves it all!

she loves make-up   & the masks it affords![1]
she loves her silver pots of rouge: the bursts of pink & red

& gold: mirrors upon mirrors: upon mirrors: she loves finding herself
at the center of a tiffany's diamond ring & wondering:

whhhhhhhat all the fuss is about ????   why are all those people complaaaaining ????

---

1 baby read anorexia websites for two years to learn the tricks of the trade. she wore lose fitting clothes, she kept her fridge empty, and
   she filled her stomach with liquids, though she never drank juice – too many empty calories. one morning, however, she indulged in
   a dozen scoops of ice-cream and the creamy mix of sugars was tastier than she'd remembered and she'd ballooned to her normal
   fatso size of XXXL within a few months.

pickkkketetetet-tttttting[2]　　　　*boyyyyycooooottttttting*　　　　*protessssttttttinggggggg*[3]

there are no picket-signs here.

　　　　there is no:　　*"rrracaiclial profilingin"*　　　no:　*"sexuaual missconductct"*

there is only:　*a golden-rimmed　　mirror of vanity　　ahhhhhh　　the mirror*

the endless mirror　　ahhhhhh　　vanity　ahhhhhh　　vaaaanity

ahhhhhhhh the things she thinks　　& never says.
she knows her parents would loathe　her secret fetish:

beneath her cabinet[4]　are boxes upon boxes: of loreal　& maybelline & clinique

---

2　mother didn't understand why baby frittered away her time with make up & curlers & perfumes, why she tried to make herself *pretttttttty*. how could baby be *pretttttttty* when she was so awfully fat? she'd become a blimp, a massive balloon – though she still frosted her nails and glossed her lips. mother didn't get it: why shuffle the cards? why square the deck?

3　baby didn't care a lick about the world. she didn't care a lick about politics or current events or global affairs. she'd read the newspaper once for social studies when she needed to research an African country. she chose "Indonesia" but later realized that she'd meant "Rhodesia," which she first thought was the name for a black girl in her chemistry class but then soon discovered it was a British colonial moniker for a country in southern Africa. *duhhhhhhhhh* baby thought.

4　baby was balding, and she applied rogaine daily for a good six months, though the regimen did little but keep eight little duckling hairs alive on the crown of her head. rogaine also gave baby a patch of coarse black hair on her chest and most importantly, it gave her a modicum of faith that some day the hair on her head might grow. baby was becoming a dude, she was becoming a man – she bent over the mirror, she pouted her lips, she applied a tube of bright lip stick (re: *cherry popping pink!*).

beneath those are: estee lauder & covergirl & revlon   & nars   & elizabeth arden...

baby believes: yes, she truly believes: there is no problem make-up cannot fix,

there is nothing   make-up cannot conceal.   not her chipped enamel tooth,

not her dime-sized mole,   both of which send bolts of fear up her thighs,[5]

through her genitals, and out her mouth each night.

make-up, baby's sure, conceals it all.

so baby lives inside the diamond,   she gazes at the mirrors.
          in the small,   gilded mirror of vanity,   there is no fear.   fear is sealed away.

instead, there is a smooth frictionless world[6]   she is certain is perfection,   she is certain

---

5   mother was a fan of Richard Simmons of the Daytime Infomercial Hall of Fame – whose cheery face and glittering smile was trapped in the faux wood panels of a television box. she loved his high-voltage energy and kind gentle voice, though what mother really hoped was for Richard to set an example for baby, whose weight was teetering at an all-time high of 385 lbs and who had recently refused mother's generous offer of four weeks at fat camp.

6   baby's favorite world was found on daytime television. she'd fallen in love with Sonny Corinthos – aka Maurice Bernard – aka the sexiest mob boss in all of Port Charles – and she'd resided in the small port city, found in sprawling lots of ABC studios which blasted its show, General Hospital, to millions of hungry female viewers. Port Charles was baby's portal to everything messy and everything sexy – addiction & AIDS & "marital rape" – ie – the bizarro blip that led Luke to rape Laura and then later marry Laura ... it all happened in Port Charles. Sonny and Brenda – Sonny and Robin – Brenda and Brenda – Brenda and Brenda – it was a carnival ride of drama & intrigue & narcissism, each airbrushed face sucking, then smacking another, daily in a pastel hue at 3 PM Eastern Standard Time in Port Charles.

will last forever: the perfection of   hard white surfaces & clean lines

& mirrors: upon mirrors upon mirrors: baby looks at baby looks at baby:
she doesn't know to ask   when she might crack.

assembly

most days, baby's mouth stayed a flat, silent line.
but on occasion she would part her lips slowly, opening
        the rose bud of her mouth:

between her lips,
there was a heaving universe

which a lion, a goat, or ship could fall into and be lost forever.

*

today was the friday assembly at saint mary's school and the schoolgirls formed neat lines in the auditorium, sweet and frosty as a tray of cupcakes. parents edged the walls, smushed to aisles, the pages of their new york times spread open like wide paper sails, their starbucks coffee cups half-drunk.

baby had written an essay entitled "transgression, silence & foucault" which had won the school wide essay contest, and today she would read her prize-winning essay. ms macintire, the principal, a butch dyke lesbian, had chosen baby's essay from a stack of twelve other essays. ms macintire had majored in women's studies at evergreen state, a department with one full-time faculty member and three eager-beaver undergraduate majors. principal mac had a fondness for exact-o-knives and in-n-out burgers and tabloid magazines which featured angelina jolie and her colorful tribe of children. in fact, two months prior, principal mac adopted an ethiopian baby who she named "virginia" after virginia woolf.

principal macintire poured bountiful praise on baby's essay: words like "masterful" and "brilliant" were written in red ink on the bottom of paper. typically baby wanted to wipe her ass with praise; praise seemed the ugly twin of blame and blame baby was quite familiar with: "brainless baby" and "regally retarded" were common epithets hurled her way, mostly by a bitchy girl named jenny lowenberg whose mother had died two years ago and whose grief had hardened into a crystalized rage that was wielded with penetrating acuity at baby.

jenny lowenberg had the mean, awesome eyes of an ice cold lake and she came to class with a different lisa frank notebook, each one more fantastic and sparkly than the next. in her hair were pink-and-white ribbon-bows and dangling from her ears were fourteen-carat gold earrings in the shape of a *J* and a *L*. jenny's lunch boxes were filled with the most delicious of foods: peanut butter and jelly sandwiches cut into four dainty triangles, crusts cut off; chocolate chip cookies with the kind of buttery dough that the other girls would trade for three butterfingers, two chocolate chunk brownies, or two lemon squares.

jenny and baby had french class together, and so there was one fifty-minute block each day when baby encountered jenny. jenny would enter class and smile politely at the french teacher mister bouchard.

"merci beaucoup, monsignor bouchard" she would say
        and then turn her back,
trot past baby and flip her middle finger.

sometimes jenny would slip a special little gift, like a used tampon or a note that said

CAN YOU READ THIS, RETARD? BABY EATS PRINCIPAL MAC'S PUSSY

*

despite the terrors
            of jenny's insults
today was baby's day: baby had won the competition

            and although she stt-t-tt-ttuttered,
            and although jenny would be sitting in the front row popping
                        her bubblicious bubble-gum, her mouth articulating a kind of focused fury
                        baby could not understand
                        nor locate the source of

            baby was determined to read her goddamn essay.

the head girl rose
and led the audience in the pledge of allegiance. the whole room dipped their heads and
folded their hands across their breasts. i pledge allegiance to the flag of the united states of
america and to the republic for which it stands – one nation, under god, indivisible, with
liberty and justice for all.

next was baby.

she walked to the stage
her patent leather mary janes chattering
            as she took to the podium. silence tightened the audience.
one mother sneezed, another sighed. the principal farted.

baby shuffled her papers, squared
and re-squared the pages

she adjusted her bonnet.

she cracked her back, rolled her shoulders,
tapped the microphone.

she gurgled some water, stood straight again.

her white bib top was crisp, starched and alert.

even the pleats of her skirt arranged themselves orderly, democratically.

baby was ready.

she gulped a big gulp.

eugenics or: "for the sake of the professional class"

baby looks @ jonny t. walker iv[1]
    & then she vomits:

what baby[2] doesn't know – but what is true

is that she's vomited
    b/c she's fearful of jonny t. & his immense testosterone

w/ch seems to swarm around him like a thick flock
    of yellow jackets, venomous & silver & ready to attack.

he's a vulturous boy, large & pink & sniffing out
    fair ladies wherever he goes.

he has a yellow tuft o hair & two big floppy ears
    & protruding out is a chest as big as a brass bird cage

---

1 jonny t. was born from a swedish family that traced its lineage back to the vikings in 11th century europe – jonny t.'s mother actually descended from a german baroness that was born amidst war-torn europe & ended up settling in sweden despite her german origins – she liked to remind people of this fact when she got drunk at the country club – *im a baronessssssssss im a baronessssssss* she would say after a few cocktails – when she wasn't crunk, she resumed being a smug-faced, tight-lipped white collar society woman who might reveal her propensity for aged gouda cheese & weekly pedicures but who, more often than not, did not like to discuss her pedigreed origins.

2 baby was lacrosse team captain, a position that she'd won b/c she'd rigged her own election – so desperate was baby for prominence & power that she'd do practically anything to be on top – even stuff the ballot with eight, nine, ten, eleven, crinkled pink tickets all with her name on them – BABY – all to ensure that she'd win.

– & sometimes baby thinks she can hear a faint tweeeeeeeeet tweeeeeeeeet of a canary
        but: she's probably just hyper-alert & it's probably just PTSD.

o o o o o o no! look @ that!

baby squeals as she gazes @ the puddle
        of gray vomit lying on the floor.

yuck! says baby.
yuck! says jonny t.

golllllllllllllllllllleeeeeeeee said baby. *o no o no o golllllllllllllleeeee*

        she rushes to the bathroom
her eyes flaring w. shame.

she hasn't vomited since tuesday when she'd devoured a carrot cake left over from her father's
holiday party & then polished off a tub of peanut butter that mother used to make cookies for
baby's lacrosse team. she'd eaten too much, so what did she do, she did what she always would do.
she'd scurried to the bathroom, stuck her finger down her throat & excavated the contents of her
stomach, which included 1 kit kat bar, 8 oreos, 4 spoon fulls of peanut butter, & ½ a carrot cake.[3]

but tuesday's puke was different than today's puke.

---

3   father had brought the cake home from the annual holiday party at the small boutique law firm where he worked part-time and made
    a modest salary of $40,000 dollars per year. he spent his extra time volunteering, and sure, volunteering was really quite womanly –
    father would organize P.T.O. bake sales & man the front desk at the vet hospital – although mother would harangue him shrieking
    in a voice so shrill it could shatter the windows: *make some money! make some goddamn money you sissy!*

tuesday's puke was *intentional*
       & today's puke is decidedly not.

she crackles w. fear.

yellow sparks fly from her ears.

her mind races @ lightning speed:

yikes-yikes-yikes-yikes-yikes-yikes-yikes-yikesssssss
       i <3 - i <3 jonny t. walker iv. – i <3 <3 <3 <3 <3[4] jonny t.

walker iv. & look @ whut ive done: grossssss upon grossssss upon grossssss
       but dat kit kat wus gooooooooooooood

maybe ill put a lil peeeeanut buddah on da kit kat
       & maybe ill add a lil strawberry jam [SMUCKERS]

omg! omg! omg! whut is wrong wit me ??????
       why am i tinkin abt addin peanut buddah & jam

2 my vomit ?????? OOOWWWWEEEEEEEEEEE

jonny t. walker iv.

---

4 baby liked to text this phrase often & many: <3 <3 jonny t <3 <3 jonny t <3 i <3 jonny t <3 i <3 jonny t <3 i <3 jonny t <3 i <3
jonny t <3 i <3 jonny t <3 i <3 jonny t <3 i <3 jonny t – one time baby put a whopping 500,000 hearts in her text message to jonny
t. – it took her a good 4½ hr to construct the message – wh/ch she did @ the expense of her algebra homework & studying for her
social studies exam – *baby i'm worried your priorities might be a little bit off* missus macintire would say to her later that week.

```
        peeks into the bathroom
throws his head back


        & laughs 2 giant laughs: LOOK @ WHUT UVE DONE
        U STUPID BABEEE
        U NASTTTTEEEEE BITCH


then jonny t. walker iv. chortles
        & coughs & cracks his knuckles


& --- *chhhhhllllllmmmppffff* --- clears his throat


& out flies a yellow wad of mucus
that lay sitting in a mass near the gastrointestinal valve at the base of the tube of his throat.


the mucus lands in baby's eye & sits there like a sty.


she says nothing.[5]
she does nothing.
she's icy. solid-
blue-as-stone.
```

---

5 after considerable research, baby had concluded that bulimia was her most effective method of weight control, for she'd tried many others: anorexia – far too difficult; laxatives – far too gaseous; enemas – far too messy – & last but certainly not least, was Vertical Banded Gastroplasty or V.G.B. – *also called The Mason Procedure or stomach stapling* – w/ch she thought might smooth out some lumps & slurp up some blub – & maybe, just maybe – mother & father might consider paying, fat as baby was – though it turned out the $25,000 dollars was too much for their bank accounts to bear – & so baby apprehended she couldn't do it – *lest she claimed disability* – & at 188 lbs – baby was really very fat, though she certainly wasn't obese & no goddamn h.m.o. was going to let poor chubby baby get one of the most expensive procedures around – & so – baby settled on bulimia, not bariatric, to solve this pernicious problem of fat.

jonny t. walker iv.[6] laughs & gallops away.

[THE END]

---

6 before there was jonny t. walker iv. – there was jonny t. iii – before there was jonny t. iii – there was jonny t. walker ii ... the question that one would then presume to follow was: who would carry on jonny t. v., vi., vii., viii. ? what fair dame would mix w. the genes of white supremacy & world domination that jonny t. would gloriously provide? it need not be a real live dame – in flesh & blood & body – she could also be an egg, provided it was the *right* egg – a "good egg" – it could all begin as a lovely cocktail, a delicate glass petri dish that shimmered & sparkled w. a good egg & little round-headed sperm that carried the chromosomes (aabdbdaabdaaabdaabb) of the Aryan Nation that the walker family so desperately wanted to propagate.

easy recipes for butterscotch lesbian treats: or "look, the gaze"

baby didn't like to be looked at, she didn't like people looking
she didn't like the idea of looking, she didn't like the idea of a look – look,
the gaze, *what was the gaze?*

she was against[1] *the very idea of the gaze*, she'd read laura mullvay,
she'd read bell hooks, she'd read catherine mackinnon, she knew –
she knew *sex was commodified,*
she knew *bodies were commodified,*
she knew it was a losing battle, what with her vagina & breasts
& her hush-puppy voice – these parts – made it all – a losing battle,[2]
she knew she would lose
she would lose
she knew she would lose her dignity,
she knew she would fall –
fall –   fall –   disappear –

---

1 baby spent a lot of time talking to her lesbian friends about what it meant to be political, what it meant to fight the system, what it meant to be queer, what it meant to be down, what it meant to be anti- (re: *anti-white, anti-man, anti- capital, anti-penis, anti-, anti-, anti-, anti-*) – she got pleasure out of this position, she got pleasure out of power, she got pleasure out of anti- & -anti- and she got power out of ideology of anti- & pleasure, pleasure & dogma, pleasure & dogs, dogs & dogma –

2 baby decided to start a club at school dedicated to feminism. she thought gender rights would be her political issue de joir – when in fact – there were issues bigger than gender rights – issues like *candy rights & avocado rights & sleep rights & labor rights* – & baby didn't know how to navigate the panoply of contradictions that seemed to emerge once she'd scratched the surface of politics & what it could mean.

under & within the gaze
within or without or inside her sex (note: *organs, gonads*)
she presumed – she felt – she was losing, losing her dignity,
losing her power, losing her authority, she would lose it,
if she surrendered to it, she was sure – she would lose it,
which is how she felt when she had to deal with all – *those looks! those looks!*

(better to avert the gaze)
(better to cast one's eyes downward)
(better to pretend you don't know – pretend you don't know anything)

it all seemed like a joke, a ruse, a trick,
the ways in which she punished[3] herself, she did – *she punished herself*
for the very things she desired

---

3 missus macintire had been the faculty advisor for the feminist club and she was responsible for baby's bad politics. she had weekly
   lunches with baby at noon where each would eat a ham sandwich & coke and missus mac would discuss what skills were needed to
   cut off a penis with a long silver knife (note: *good gag reflexes, crystalline rage*).

(she desired[4] looks???) (she desired looks[5]?!?!? whhhhaaat?!?!?!) (she desired looks from menns?!?!?) (looks from womenss???!?!?!!!) (looks & attentions?!?!? anntenstions & not-to-mentions??) (whaaaattt then of mennnns??!?!?) (i thought baby was a lesbian!!! omg omg omg – she's not a lesbian feministss!?!?!? omg omg omg – she's not – she's not?!?!?! omg omg omg – she was never ever a lesbian?!?!?) (how could she not – if she's wom-man & wom-man-ly & angry – how could should be anything but a lesbian?!?!?!) (duhhhhhhh she's a lesbian duhhhhhhhhh she's a lesbian but she doesn't know she's a lesbian – duhhhhhhhhhh –)

baby's like totally like totally like totally not the feminist[6] she thinks she is she's not at all the lesbo she thinks she is she's not she's not

---

4 missus macintire introduced baby to ideologies of lesbian feminism & anti-capitalism that made baby hate her own body & its strange pleasures and sensations – sensations which erupted inside her as she peeped on johnny t. walker iv. naked late one night. *she thought she was bad, she thought she was wrong* – she thought she was violating the sacrosanct doctrine of lesbian feminism and thus violating herself – baby could not make sense of the (note: -*homo*, -*hetero*, -*pan*) desires which surged within her and she was certain missus macintire couldn't either. (note: baby was right – missus macintire would eject baby from the feminist club within a few short hours of finding erotica written by baby which featured far too much cock and far too little fisting than missus macintire thought was appropriate for anyone under her guidance.)

5 baby had fantasies of being raped, and she didn't know how to reconcile these fantasies with her new position as president of her high school feminist club. she had recently acquired a girlfriend & a buzz cut & a sincere belief in the transformational power of lesbian feminism. how then could she explain the rape dreams? how could she qualify them? she dreamed her buttocks red & raw one night where johnny t. walker iv. smashed her window, broke into her house, tied her down and smacked her around. he then screwed her relentlessly for hours, his cock so prodigious, a nasty snarl fixed on his mouth – oh, she got wet from the thought.

6 *baby had fantasies of rape, but she also protested against rape.* she petitioned congress w. anti-rape bills, she'd offered her own testimony, she'd offered her own story. she fought fiercely for survivors – and also her own survival – and she balanced her own colorful rape fantasies w. equally ardent attempts to eradicate rape. *it didn't make sense – or maybe it did?* baby would spend a whole decade in analysis w. doctor goodall before she'd understood the origin of her desire (re: *political, sexual*) and then when she found it – *whooooosh* – it quickly disappeared. *baby had fantasies of rape, and she also protested against rape*, doctor goodall wrote in her notes. *did it need to make sense?* (note: it did and didn't, it could and it couldn't.)

she saw johnny t. looking at the vids – she saw johnny t. looking at the vids
of her (baby!) – (naked!) – & she was like whoooooooooooooa –
she was like whooooooaaaaa – baby – was like whooooooooaaaaa
dats kinda hottttt[7]
(& then she was like: whooooaaaa)
(whoaaaa) i thought a was a- / supposed – to be / a- / ball-busting /
balllll- busting – feminist[8]-   but–

then why do i want to get down on the floor & crawl
w/ four legs & suck a pacifier & chew on a carrot & then ride you like a horseeeeee)
(why do i want to do that / do that / if i'm like soooooooooooo political?[9])
(if i'm like suuuuuch a lesssssbian / lessssbobobo) (([[*side note*: baby

---

7 *baby first discovered sadomasochism as a child* – it was something doctor goodall would realize years into daily analysis – after baby
   had spooled out a strange story in a fit of exhaustion; it was not something doctor goodall had expected – although she was, in fact,
   quite titillated. she nudged baby to say more – baby had stumbled upon the thrill of spanking at age twelve – johnny t. trembled &
   baby had assumed the position of domme – she slid in so easily, the role fit like a glove. she made him drop to his knees, she pulled
   out a whip. baby hadn't known the words for it, but there it was – *power and its infinite pleasures.*
8 baby had tried to delineate the varieties of feminism on her first day of feminist club. it was not an easy task because each branch
   of feminism splintered off to create a whole other branch which then fractured again in a million different directions. (example:
   feminine feminism & faux feminism & freaky feminism & fucking! feminism – & those were simply the "f" feminisms – there were
   also more legitimate forms of feminism, like *lesbian feminism & transfeminism & black feminism & marxist feminism* & & &...)
   she wrote them on the green chalkboard; it looked like civil war inside a rectangular wood frame.
9 baby hadn't yet learned that feminist ideology could never be bound – the wide, wild tracts of experience much more lush than the
   fence of identity theory – which would always collapse on itself, always contradict itself – baby had come to feminism looking for
   refuge, looking for salvation. *she had come looking to reconcile the contradictions within her desires, not knowing that feminism
   would bring her deeper into the forest.* (note: the forest was dark and green. the ticks burrowed in her vagina, but she no longer called
   the organ by the name "vagina." she instead called it "mistress macintire" – she wanted to honor the high priestess of her pussy and
   its infinite possibilities.)

said once, "I'm a Lavender Lesbian on Mondays
& I'm a Furry Unicorn on Tuesdays
& I'm a Butterscotch Bisexual Bottom on Thursdays"]]
& don't you know / don't you know / it was all true –
it was all true – except she switched up the days
& the flavors & she was kind of some (or none) of those things.)

an untitled invective

baby wrote from anger, it was really quite simple. she liked to talk about writing for *"justice"* or *"survival"* or *"redemption"* or *"political resistance"* but she wrote, really, from a deep red fury that boiled in her veins and spilled out on the page in the form of long bloody sentences with names she'd later xxxxx out and then xxxxx then she'd draw little daggers on the margins of the text

pointing to terms like *"white supremacy"* & *"imperialism"* & *"cis-hetero-patriarchy"* –

but she never ever pointed at herself and her own guilty heart.

she could point at terms & gather language – oh, there is *"cis-gender"*!

– oh, there is *"heteronormative"*!   – oh, there is *"subalternity"*!

        oh, there is *"Angela Davis' analysis / of the prison industrial complex"*!

but she never looked within, she never looked within language,

        she never looked within herself.

she approached *"politics"* & *"identity"* from the outside,
as something separate from her body –
she never filled its spacious rooms, so she never knew them
& never knew how to inhabit them, how to refuse them, how to leave them –

she thought she needed to look somewhere outside, somewhere – *out there* –
somewhere, over the rainbow (note: enter scarecrow, snatch ruby slippers.)
& not dead-center in the middle of her body, in the middle of her belly.

she couldn't look within, she didn't know how –
she didn't know how to listen, she only knew how to look.

she saw herself only as *a spectacle*, only as *an object*
only as *a subjected object*, only as *a subject-object-verb-agreement*—
who never articulated what she really wanted to say
      who never authored language
who never authorized language,
      but one who was instead authored by language.

what then? what could she do?

she didn't control anything, she didn't control money,
she didn't control sexxxxx, she didn't control language,
and she certainly didn't control where her language landed, if it landed anywhere.
(note: where *did* her words land? did they land on ears? on paper?
on pixelated computer screens? did her words lie dead, flat
on the page?)

baby didn't realize that she wrote *inside* language
when she wrote inside anger – *she was angry, god damn it!* – she had a lot to be angry about.

anger was something she could stand inside,
although it was also something she couldn't quite know – she couldn't quite language –

she refused the anger she knew so intimately –
she refused anger & in favor of high-minded ideas

about "*Art*" & "*Politics*" – ideas like –

"indeterminacy" & "post-structuralism"
& an art-like fondue of / Great & Powerful Ideas To Shape The Nation.

baby instead wanted to write clean philosophical proofs
with the cool blue hand of objectivity.

she didn't want to write knotty invectives in bright red ink,
invectives came easily to baby, though invectives

were ideas empty of intellect, empty of rigor –
ideas bloated by feelings – *eeeeewwwww* – feelings

such Embarrassing, Inelegant Things.

ARTIFACTS (1973) AND ENDNOTES (2999)

the nutrient value of dog food was really quite high – higher than most meals baby ate;
 for most meals she ate were: ketchup mixed w. chocolate sauce
or occasionally a basket of oreos, battered & fried –
 but really, what baby was attempting to do[i]
was free herself from food – in all forms –
 & in this, she attempted to free herself
from *Desire* – & its menacing grandchild: *Craving*
 though *Craving's* lovely sister, *Suffering*
sat in the corner, shimmering & blonde & slumped
 like any good-girl-emo-hipster[ii] should
& although doctor goodall often told baby that eating
 disorders were not "white girl problems"[iii]
she had a hard time accepting this; b/c she came from African / slaves
 & slave ships & she knew hunger
much greater than calorie counting: she knew lack, she knew want:
 wanting freedom, wanting love,[iv] wanting
some goddamn *privacy*,[v] some goddamn *decency*,[vi] wanting
 a moment alone in The Rose Garden
w.o. the bright U.V. lights of Double Consciousness[vii]
 and DuBois' head tucked between two sad professors' asses,[viii]
crammed there – wedged between African-
 American-Studies and Corporate-Social-Responsibility;
each bloke looks so dapper in his Brooks Brothers suit

& so very slick – so very "H-H-H-H-A-R-V-A-R-D" (T.M.)
as they espouse The Truth[ix] Of The Black Experience,[x]
wrapped in silver + gold & fed: To A Great White Shark.

~ written by baby

i   "we all deal with the problems of the world differently. sometimes it's through eating. sometimes it's through not eating..." she would write in her diary, one of 4,000,000 notebooks all stacked in the back corner of the basement that the authorities would find many years after the crime, beside her remains, her gnawed out body, dead – though alive and teeming with gnats and ants, traipsing through, breeding & building their own little animal kingdom. the notebooks bore witness to her suffering, even when others refused to bear it themselves (re: *parents, psychiatry, society*).

ii   *it's not a joke*, doctor goodall said. *rape and bulimia are not jokes.*
        they're not rinky-dink slapstick routines
    you can hop, skip & jump out of –
        no joke will absolve the fact of your suffering,
    no joke will erase the reality of it.

iii   miss mac gave her foucault and foucault gave her form; form gave her language where before she had none, a vast clean expanse on which she built all sorts of lies. first, there was the false belief she was better than rape and better than women who had no language for rape. then later, the thick black lines of form and anti-form would separate *oregon* from *idaho*, *no* from *i don't know*, *pleasure* from *pressure*, and other troubling words.

iv   she believed she could always go back to the drawing board, pick up the pens – pick up the quill & the knife – & re-write her story: re-write the history of rape & abuse – *shhhhh* – & re-write the lies & betrayals and all that – she believed that in writing her own story & writing her own poems & anti-poems, she might solve her problem, might erase her own history. she could dot her *i*'s and cross her *t*'s and mark the page with *x*'s and *o*'s ...

and create some sort of world much greater than her own small dollhouse,
     w. its maze of tiny corridors and silver spoons.

v   ... she wrote poems & fictions & stories;
          she wrote diaries & articles & love letters never sent & imitation poems
               & lists & descriptions of mama-bear & papa-bear & baby-bear;

     ... she wrote the kind of world she dreamed herself inside,
          the kind of world she needed to escape to ...

     she wrote sweeping epics w. corseted maidens & galloping horses
          & burly cowboys & jenny lowenberg's occasional appearance,

     where jenny wanders onto the horizon of the text,
          tiptoes onto the surface of the page, and smacks the maiden,
               steals her cowboy, runs off w. the loot and out of the story ...

vi the truth was almost no one had baby's interests at heart – not her mother, not her father, not
    miss mac, certainly not her stepdad. each was caught in their own matrix of rationalization
    – *but there are reputations at stake, but there's money involved* – which they bandied about
    like expert attorneys, not parents, not protectors. the truth was the only person who cared a
    lick about baby was bertha, baby's nanny of ten years who raised her from 4 to 14. bertha left
    when the allegations surfaced – and then saw baby once more, three years later, from behind
    the plexi-glass window of a pick-up truck: baby, 17, stood on the corner of mount olympus,
    nibbled on a marlboro and negotiated the price of fellatio with a cop. bertha sat, silent – hands
    gripped on the wheel, ready to rush out of the car and onto the street and pluck baby away.

what could she do? she loved her, but what could she do? she sat and watched. she shook – her whole body shook. after five minutes, she drove away.

vii   "the nutrient value of dog food" was the poem baby most loved for it reminded her of a baroque robo-tripping hawaiian holiday she might want to take. the poem was kooky in the way baby was kooky: in the way baby was not in control of her own chaotic fury, which bounced around & wreaked a sort of havoc, she could neither recognize nor understand. the poem failed, and baby believed the poem failed, if she believed anything at all, because she herself had failed. she said these words one morning in english class, coming off meth, though still believing in language & her own pompous proclamations – *the poem fails, not because it lacks language,* she said, *but because it lacks depth.*

viii   there were four years during baby's childhood where she had frequent erotic dreams about bertha, and where baby woke up w. her clitoris wet & cherry-red & throbbing; the dreams were not outlandish, given baby's age and trauma history. she'd forged a close relationship with bertha and the emotional intimacy that she'd found w. bertha soon collapsed into a desire for sexual intimacy, as well. what often emerged were sex dreams where bertha's vague outline enveloped her body & brought her down into a dark, spicy mix of lesbian-sex and labor-kink dirty talk –

o   o   o   o   o   ! ! !   bbb-b u t-t-t

– tttttt-er my buuuutler! butttttter my butler!

bertha sensed baby had a crush on her and she gently closed the door on any possibilities for romance, professional that she was. she declined baby's offers for sleepovers and movie-dates and once – when baby had come home high – for the simple exchange of fifty dollars for a full body oil & hot stone massage, undies off.

ix   im eatin dog food.
oh.
can i have sum?

alternate ending
im eating dog food.
oh.
dats gross.
now i need 2 spank u.

den spank me mama.
den spank me.

x   the detective concluded that the poem "the nutrient value of dog food" was not, in fact, written in 1973. it had been written, instead, in 1933 or 1966 – depending on the radiocarbon dating of papyrus and whether the detective was snorting coke the day he descended into the laboratory and fiddled with the liquid scintillation counter. no matter the difference, no matter his habit – once he discovered that the poem was a facsimile, a dummy poem – the detective would furiously declare to his colleague, bull-nostrils a-flare: *the poem is a hoax! baby never wrote it!* then his colleague rubbed his goatee, sighed and paused before asking 3 prize-winning questions: 1. *well then, who wrote it?* 2. *who is baby?* 3. *what is baby trying to hide?*

THEORY AND KOOL-AID

it's always the most boisterous cock-suckers, the ones who let you know how many dicks they had in their mouth the previous night – those ones were also – *always!* – a total bore, a total – *snnnnnnore*, bore – and jonny t. walker iv. used sex & erotics to prop himself up and make him more interesting than he actually was.

jonny t. popped dicks like tic tacs though he was really a dud – his interior life was really quite hollow – built around the illusion that people might love him and love to fuck him – when in fact they didn't, not really – or they did – but they didn't love him – they didn't even really enjoy him, not all that much – jonny t. was just another expendable body, though he liked to believe otherwise – he liked to live in an interminable fantasy – a merry-go-round where he'd cum & cum & cum & endlessly cummmmm – he'd lie on a waterbed and get hammered by a three fingered porn star named Jerry Lowenberg who recently had a sex change (F to M) and had once curtsied and called herself Jenny Lowenberg, as she entered the text / as she entered baby's text.

it seemed like a joke, a bogus proposition – all this queer theorizing – what did it matter? why did she care? — *homo- or hetero- or bi-love?* — *erotic sex or not-sex? romantic friendship or lite fondling?* — she wanted to refine each category to its very essence – she wanted to sort & define & delineate – *femme-man or wom-man or womxn?* – such categories, such language seemed like baby's only entrance into a field of study that had long excluded her – *a subject she'd felt both seduced by and profoundly alienated by*, she had written once and then forgotten.

a clean ivory queer love (re: *trans love* re: *eros*) was something she'd never known – not in life, not in fantasy, not in sex. baby had not known any of it – *feminism & white women, white wommenss & love* – it confounded her – *queer love or homo-romantic?* – *gay sex or femme desire?* – baby hadn't the language for it, she was too black, she was too bland, she was too lonely – baby was lonely, she was very lonely. sure, she had skirted around the edges of some kinds of love, some of the categories she obsessed over but never fully encountered – *homo- or hetero- or bi-love? romantic friendship or lite fondling?* – but she wanted to know true love, she wanted to do more than bump up against its edges, in theory and in life – but she'd never known the real thing in its pure form.

she wanted it, marked by the hands of capitalism
she wanted her body, marked by the hands of capitalism
she wanted them this way, she wanted them – turn her this way

madam capitalism, mama capitalism

(madam capitalism said) (she said) (she said) (baby was sloppy) (sloppy and lazy and often uncouth) (she said) (mama capitalism said) (she burped a lot) (she scratched her crotch at all the wrong times) (she never answered email) (she never said things right) (madam capitalism said) (she said) (she was rude & impatient) (she was bad w. bureaucracy) (she had no manners) (example) (example) (give me an example) (she didn't do the project) (she didn't clean her room) (she didn't wash the dishes) (macaroni crusted on the bowl) (pizza lay face down on the floor) (a patch of fungus lined the china) (it grew, it grew) (it grew into a big leafy tree) (the tree exploded from the plate) (the plate which lay in the sink) (the sink which lined the counter) (the plate, the sink, the counter) (none of it mattered) (why did it matter) (each had devolved into a state of disorder) (internal disorder meets external disorder) (disorder rejoinder) (disorder reorder) (disorder mama capitalism could not have fathomed) (she fathomed, she could not fathom) (baby could trim it) (could baby trim it) (had she the clippers) (where were the clippers) (where were the clippers) (she couldn't find the clippers) (where were they) (where were they) (there was fungus on her plate) (she lied down on her bed) (she began to clip) (clip clip clip) (oh – ooooh no, ooooh) (oh whoooa – oh – oh) (it wasn't exactly an orgasm) (clip clip clip) (it wasn't exactly) (clip clip clip) (it didn't last very long) (it was more like a quick, a rapid – a something?) (a paroxysm?) (a spasm?) (and then it was done) (it was done) (baby was done) (baby had unraveled) (the kitchen had unraveled) (then her pubes did too) (no, loosened) (wait, atrophied) (no, no – not that) (not that) (she wanted a smooth clean look) (she wanted them smooth) (she wanted them clean) (she didn't want a wild forest) (down there) (down there) (down where) (down there)

a defanged baby beluga cat-loving wom-man

baby believed if she was to gain any success –
she needed to become a sort of *defanged baby beluga cat-loving woman* ...

who never said anything to piss people off –
who never said anything worth more than a cup of yogurt (re: *strawberry, yoplait*)

who never claimed any sort of position, took any sort of stance about
       "art" or "non-art" or "not-art" or "capital(ized) art"...

the problem was baby was baby –
she was not *a defanged baby beluga cat-loving woman* ...

she was just an arrogant artist
who justified her snobbery with a growing body of work,

which she was sure the whole universe would love
though it didn't work out that way, of course –

she never showed anything.
she never sold anything.
she never made anything –

     just scratches on the surface of time ...

baby avoided the questions about whether her work was art
(note: *it wasn't.*)

as she avoided the questions about whether her work was good
(note: *it wasn't.*)

    ... & baby avoided these questions with torpedo attacks on everyone else's work[1]

she used *the logic of anti-racism-anti-ablism-anti-capitalism*
       to make a case for *the erasure of a lifetime of words and images*
she had never made in the first place –

but *the logic of anti-racism doubled over*[2]
into a case she made for
her own inability to make art
her own incapacity to participate
in the structures she sought to destroy.

---

1 it was fascinating the extent to which baby would extrapolate outwards, "money issues" = *capitalism*, "sex issues" = *patriarchy*, "food issues" = *corporate media*, etc etc. missus macintire had indoctrinated baby in a flavor of Critical Race Theory where baby abdicated personal responsibility & placed it on the marble mantle of White Supremacy, White Supremacy baby secretly imagined would one day wipe her ass & clean her shit & & place her in a tiny gilded cage, where she'd nibble on long stemmed carrots w. wide green leaves & sink deep into a featherbed – where she imagined she was free, where she imagined she was empty.

2 yes, baby had "art issues," but *art was merely a reflection of the world inside her mind*; "art" was no different from the rest of the world, just as "baby" was no different from the rest of the world: "art" = "politics" = "religion" = "anything else" = *"art" was stupid & "baby" was stupid* ... & *people were stupid*, but baby didn't really realize this, baby didn't see this ... & so: *baby couldn't outwit art / or outthink art / or booby trap her way towards an "art life" / where she would / could be free of "art issues."*

... the truth was baby wasn't sure / if she *could* destroy power
& baby wasn't sure / if she *should* destroy power

    ... because she wasn't sure, really, if she held power.

baby was caught in a matrix of rationalization
about the systems she was a part of – *racisms – isms – or&-sexixisssmms –&or-classsisism*
–or&-heterosex—issms—or—ismss&-issms-or-&ismmmms

baby believed these systems defined her
& *she was convinced she could not de-fine or de-fang or re-define them...*

it was this ambivalence / it was this uncertainty / about the systems she lived within
and couldn't imagine herself without (*racism, she was in love with racism!*) (*sexism, she was in*
love with sexism!) which kept her chained to the system –

kneeling before it
humping it like a pathetic dog
as she declared proudly

oh so proudly! *imma ... rrrrrrrrraddddiccccalllll*[3] ...

baby grew angrier as she grew lazier.

      & she was consumed w. rage about the lives & follies of those around her
... instead of the raw material inside her / the material in front of her / the clay sitting
alone and lonesome on the table / the paints waiting patiently in the pots ...

what it was, really, was baby [4] (it wasn't -racisms – or&-sexisms -&-or-classisms – or-
&-heterosexisms-) *it was baby*: it was baby's mushrooming criticism / criticism of self-
/ & criticism of others / baby's -self-critique / robust (self)-examination – then – too –
her self-abasement / (in a basement) – *it consumed her, it paralyzed her* ...
baby rattled off the failures of others / so she could avoid her own inveterate failures,
which she was sure of, which she also couldn't avoid,

---

3 baby was constantly broke and constantly angry – and she thought she had to be angry in order to be *rrrrraaddical*. the fight wasn't
    worth it, but she wasn't quite ready to give up. she found too much comfort in the idea that she was *standing on the right side of*
    history, she found too much comfort in *the illusion of moral superiority*, and so she didn't realize that she might possibly be *wrong*.
    she might be *right* about capitalism, but she might be *wrong* about herself and her position within the whole enterprise, her position
    within the machine. baby thought she stood outside it, when she stood at its very center. she thought by raging against the system,
    she thought she was somehow removed from it. it was no wonder she pounded away and she found herself tired. she was pounding
    on air.

4 baby had "art issues," which were similar to baby's "food issues" & then also baby's "money issues" & also baby's "sex issues."
    baby had "issues." baby had "issues" / which really had nothing to do with "art" or "money" or "sex" or whatever else *she might*
    describe and thus circumscribe, which is to say – *baby used "x issue" to construct an elaborate story / at the center of which she bore*
    absolutely no responsibility / she claimed absolutely no misdeed – all those "art issues" & "money issues" & "sex issues" – baby
    had "issues," all right – she had issues with herself, she really didn't like herself, that's all.

she avoided her own inveterate failings (sloth, malice, jealousy) *w. a thorough examination of the failures of others –*

("jenny lowenberg & the conspiracy of jewey late capitalism") ("johnny t. walker iv. & the triumph of white supremacy in the supposedly liberal age of pokemon ... or is it ... bugs bunny?? ... or is it ... hannah montana??" etc etc etc...)

it was hard to distinguish between baby's criticism of others & her criticism of self;

it all seemed inter-connected / re-connected / -const-ructed /-self = other = doctor
goodall = which was which? & she couldn't distinguish – she couldn't
see her 1, 2, 3, or 4 selves,[5] she couldn't see –
2 comes-before-3

the (inner) critics said: baby didn't know how to write – the (inner) critics said:
she was *illiterate* – she was *lazy* – she was *over-determined* – she took *all the wrong risks* –

in all the *wrong places* she was *afraid of beauty* – she was   *afraid of love*
the (art) critics said: the (art) critics said: if she could be more *arty* –

_____

5 baby found herself torn between doctor goodall & miss macintire, torn between the dogma each woman espoused (re: *psychiatry*)
(re: *critical race theory*) – baby was pulled between the two women, in lieu of a mother who neglected baby, in lieu of a mother
who revealed herself only in absence – doctor goodall offered baby the cold attention & tyrannical dignity of a matriarch, miss
macintire offered long-winded diatribes about capitalist-hetero-patriarchy – they were comforting, in a way – in the way the
diatribes offered a conviction that baby had never known in her own childhood.

if she could be less *esoteric* – if she could be *more commercial* – *more relaxed* –

a little less highbrow – *a little less constipated* – just a little looser –   if she could just –
take a shit – if she could just loosen: her stools –   if she could just neuter   the dog
– *if she could just neuter* –

if she could neuter the dog
if she could neuter herself
if she could neuter her work

if she didn't constantly reference reams & reams of art
theory – if she didn't *always talk about race*
if she didn't *always talk about power*[6] – if she could do all that –

then art audiences would love her
then the art critics would love her
& she'd be complete in her snobbery –

      & she'd be both violently hated[7] *& passionately adored* –

---

6 "accountability" and "agency" and "claiming ownership" – these were some the late-capitalist words doctor goodall used as she
tried to make baby see, as she tried to keep baby alive. the words appeared to certain readers as an obvious neoliberal hack, and
who likes that – *eeeewwwww* – (note: insert new modifier, cherry flavored) the truth was doctor goodall was not a pompous prep
who wore boat shoes and shetland sweaters – she didn't spend summers in maine, she didn't go camping for fun – no, no, she wasn't
white-bred like that – *doctor goodall was down, doctor goodall was woke* – she was a capitalist-psychiatrist and also a life coach – a
la Tony Robbins – and she believed in the stunning singularity of individualism.

7 baby was smothered in loathing, she couldn't see her own internalized core – she was a wet swarmy booger child, she satiated her
own vulva – she curled inward, she bowed like a fetus, she was a fetus, she was feral, she was fecund – she turned to herself for her
own sick forms of pleasure because *she refused to ask for it straight up, diet coke with ice, please.* she was a pervert, what could she
say? she loved to do weird things with her body and she loved to ask others to do them too. jenny lowenberg called her a creep and
baby didn't want to be bad, she didn't want jenny to think she was baaaaaaad.

3 follow(ed)-by 4
(baby had become an art snob) (uggggghhhh)
(she was kind of an art snob who hated art) (shakespeare? uuuggggghhhhhh)
(picasso? grrossssssss) (bethoveen? sssnnnnooooorrree) (manet? boooringinggging)

(note: *art snobs hated art, right? that's what made them snobs, right? they had an imperious disdain for all they saw. nothing could be good enough, nothing could satisfy their impossibly delicate palates — a little salt in the caviar, eh? a sprig of mint in the crème freche, eh? eh?*)

4 afterward-s or 5
[*applause. clap. clap. tomatoes are thrown on stage.*] [*piano thrown into audience. legs break and smash.*]
[*an elderly man bleeds. more cheers. more riots.*]
[*tomato juices run down piano legs.*]

channel 7: or "true story"

the day of the beauty pageant was one whole week after jenny lowenberg's mother had died in a tragic car accident on route 66. jenny had been in the car and there were no injuries for jenny, except a fleshy pink scar that traveled up her right thigh and would remain with her the rest of her life. her mother had perished in an instant, dead before the paramedics arrived.

jenny had used the moment of her mother's death and the platform of the beauty pageant to give an impassioned speech about the importance of family, the passage of time and the fragility of life. this was after, of course, jenny had twirled her baton, strutted the stage in a silver leotard and gold lamé heels and tap danced in front of a panel of eight ogling men, a transsexual named joseph, and a gender-nonconforming straight woman (re: *femmenazi*) who was writing an expose on scandals within beauty pageants in the wake of jonbenet ramsey's death. (note: the expose never got published because the chauvinist editors at Random House refused to look at the manuscript, laughing & grinning & gawking when they saw its asinine title – *beauty & po-mo heter-normative dialectics within georgia's beauty pageant culture*.)

there were also ten other contestants in the pageant:
meow-meow gabor
     lana turner
        afreeka white
           tabitha smiley
              cookie roberts
                  princess mattel
                     chiquita banana
                        philomena donahue

each presented their stories
      & swished their bottoms
w. a great deal of glory.

the judges spent twenty minutes deliberating.

they went through the list & tallied up the scores (note: *turner, av. 12.78; white, av. 17.99; roberts,
av. 13.67 mattel, av. 12.53; av. 18.01; banana, av. 4.99; donahue, av. 5.41; harassme, av. 15.88;
tiara, av. 15.67*)
      & when they came to the end, they found they'd had a triple tie.

smiley, av. 18.9999
gabor, av. 18.9999
lowenberg, av. 18.9999

the judges spoke @ length about meow-meow,
      they spoke @ length about tabitha

& then they spoke @ length about jenny:

they considered jenny's story, they considered her tragedy.
they considered her ass, they considered her smile.
they considered her crocodile tears
      which she pinched out of her eyes
            which fell to the floor like three freshly cut diamonds.

they considered
        & considered
     & considered ...

& then finally, the judges considered the network's tv producers,

who sat in a row behind the curtains (re: *backstage left – behind the flower pots sipping dunkin donuts coffee*).

the producers spoke into the judges' ear pieces with syrupy-smooth voices
and said the following:

... well, we've got a cat or a jew-girl or a black-girl
     & i must say:
we better go with the cat.
     a cat is a helluva-lot smarter than those two hoes combined.

[snap. click off.]

primordial history

(in da land bf time der wus a chile born
from a giant dinosaur egg & dis chile
had 3 legs & 5 fingers & 2 very fat lips
dis chile spoke loud i say dis chile wus
l o q u a c i o u s dis chile wouldn't stop
talkin as a matter o fact she wus a bit o
a motor mouth yessuh yessuh she wus
yesssuh her lips a pink blur yessuh
dis in da lan bf time)

"act like a lady"

act 1

oh daddy look a here. der is ketshup
& fluffer-nuttter on da carpet. oh
daddy whud shud we do? [silence.]
i dunno, why u askin me lil bitch
clean up ur own goddamn mess.
[silence. long silence.] waaa-waaa
stop crying. goddamnit please
stop crying.

act 2

[baby leans over & spills coffee on
the carpet] o-oh oh-oh o-o-oh
sigh. lemme run & get a feather
duster & a broom-stick & wet rag.
ill scrub her down real gud daddy.
reeeeal reeeal gud daddy.

u like it real clean rite
real clean

untitled ampersand

& she's vulnerable. / & she's written something real. / & she calls herself a poet.

    & she's christened w. a title

she ½ loves & ½ loathes & walks about her days

in starry-eyed confusion, wasting words / wasting poetry, wasting the raw material

of her life – for fun & fuchsia, masks & cloaks, tricks & pots / she's wastes it

    all for poetries   *presshious poettreiess*

or so says *baby* or so says *the speaker* or so says *the author* –

"the true criminal is language."

& the narrator writes in invisible ink & constructs invisible cities

& the reader roams around them (*yes, you do!*) & might see maybe a problem

with baby (*if the reader is dumb*) or (*if the reader is smart*) the reader can read language –

w. remarkable x-ray eyes that scorch the invisible ink
    & render it seen – bright pink & alive

the reader would see the invisible ink

the seams within the text
    the red threads loose in the story

where invisible plots unfold / geometric & metallic
and the reader would see the construction of baby
as clearly as she sees the construction of language
as a problem not of baby

but a problem of society & sandcastles
    & the cities which made baby, a problem

of subtext, a problem of
    narration, a problem of
representation, a problem of Language

which can only be solved by Language herself –

but Language chooses not to solve the problem.
Language chooses to be lazy,
propped up on the couch / eating oreos & watching jerry springer
while the reader & writer & characters –
are all left hanging by a long slim cord;
they are all left waiting for Language to
address the problem of power,
the problem of history, the artifice of it all,
waiting for Language to sign
her name, finally to the document ...

_____

[Sign Here]

parabola

"the typical totems of ordinary success"

baby didn't want to accrue
       the typical totems of ordinary success (*love, language, money*)

she wanted only to surrender –
       although this was a lie – she told herself –

on days she thought writing was a noble pursuit
       and not the hack job it really was (*this was language, was this language*)

baby would enter a literary world[1]
which was driven by status, controlled by money –
she would enter a world where –

     there were no real writers, only Literary Entrepreneurs

only ghost writers, only ghosts,

---

1 there were the rulz of money (*turn a profit$*) there were the rulz of love (*be kind*) there were the rulz of art (*make beauty*) (*make truth*) there were the rulz of sex (*make pleasure*) (*get off*) – but the rulz seemed to contradict each other – it seemed impossible to do any of this – *be kind?!? > make beauty?!? > make truth?!? > turn a profit$$* – it seemed impossible to follow the rulz of art without breaking the rulz of money – impossible to follow the rulz of sex without breaking the rulz of love – no one could win – no one could win – baby couldn't win – each rule, the rulz cancelled out each other – constantly – *there was no value, where was value* – no value in following one set of rulz – since it cancelled out a whole – other set of rulz – though one rule – The Rulz Of Money (*turn a profit$$*) seemed to Trump all –

only ghosts of a capitalism so pernicious it hollowed out

    the spirits of all who sought artistic union with the divine ...

        & baby was divine, god damn it!
        baby was divine!

jenny lowenberg
didn't want to be a writer, *not a real writer*
only A Celebrated Public Figure, only a bronze statue –

& baby didn't want to be a bronze statue
which stood in the courtyard of A Particular Ivy League University
only to get pissed on by drunk frat kids walking by ...

    why would she want to be that kind of writer?

writing seemed less about turning a phrase
& more about kissing up to young editors,

who expected to receive the same goodies

they were offered before they took the masthead –
    blow-jobs for internships; anal for book contracts[2] –

love too was another source of confusion, often just as transactional as art –
love was an exchange, it demanded response, recompense.
it was conditional, it depended on something being done.
something had to be done! something had to be done, goddamn it!
baby needed to *do* something.
she needed to *be* something, in order to be loved,

she needed to be pretty, she needed to be kind ...

    but oh how she secretly wished, she wished
she wished! to lie in a fetal position on a stained grey carpet, watch television
and eat cool ranch doritos ...

    – oh, how she secretly wished to be ordinary!

        oh, how she secretly wished to be ordinary! –

---

2 *rulz or no rulz* – she would need to dispense with the rulz – dispense w. obedience, dispense w. morality, dispense w. order –
dispense w. all things sacred and pure – *rulz or no rulz* – she'd need to surrender to a chaos she didn't think she could handle – *rulz
or no rulz* – it didn't make sense; baby had grown up in a good family, she tucked in her butt & smoothed out her hair & scribbled
in her notebook. then she gave her said notebook to the Right Agent and then the Right Publisher and then the Right Editor (re:
The Right Publishers! The Right Agents! The Right Editors! – all listed in Art Rulz Handbook, page 69) and she believed she might
actually win! she'd win – she might win! – *if she followed the rulz* – she believed she might actually not die –

she wanted to live low-brow, but maintain high-class tastes.
she wanted to get ccccrrrrruunnk at the party,
flirt w. The Blacks & The Gays, then go home
and live a respectable, civilized life
with her husband-til-death mister johnny t. walker iv. ...

no, there was no divorce in the cards – no, no

     no, baby couldn't refuse the status a white man offered her –

no, she couldn't say no –
     no, she just couldn't say no, she couldn't –
despite johnny t.'s inveterate cheating,
despite his cock
being rammed up the butthole of Every Blasian Man East of the Mississippi –

baby couldn't say no,
no, she couldn't, she couldn't –

oh, how she secretly wished to live a kind of rosy gentrified fantasy life
where low-wage work wasn't an awful trap
filled with daily indignities – *no, no, not that, it wasn't that –*

though her lovers' poverty was extreme & unbearable, she refused to see it,
she refused to believe it – she refused, she refused

she refused the corollary between white buns & sacred cows,
between small toilets & hot sex –   because baby liked to fuck the people
she liked to fuck (*trailer trash queens, butchy black bois, hood rich homies*)

because, because, because
because   the sex was good & it was hot & she wanted it
like she wanted it, goddamn it!

she refused, she refused,
she refused[3] to consider the lives of her lovers, she refused – refused
– she refused to consider their pain –

because, because, because
because?   *baby couldn't contend with the ways injustice was intimate & grinding*

because, because, because
because?   *baby couldn't love under power, because baby couldn't love–*

baby couldn't love –

---

3 baby wasn't sure if she'd won or if she'd lost – she wasn't sure where she stood – by the end of the game – she'd refused to follow the rulz (*of art, of language, of love*) – although she was treasonous in all the wrong ways – she was treasonous in love (*she was gay, she was fat, she was constantly lonely*) – she was treasonous in language (*she was sentimental, she was angry, she was usually mute*) – she was treasonous in all the ways that made *treason actually criminal, not merely aesthetic* – (re: ornamental re: the kind self-styled hipsters used re: vain revolutionaries who rested, at the end of a long day, on a bed of their own making – *and refused the exile which was inevitable for all true traitors.*)

Post-Script[4] – OR? a Limp Resurrection, an – Insurrection

baby turned a blind eye
because she was a rich bitch, *a spoiled brat –*

who didn't care a lick about *fidelity* or *morality* or *decency.*
she didn't think much of her lovers
beyond their capacity to flick her clit
in a particular way which *made her cum so hard she thought she might actually die –*

yes, baby was stupid in a way only rich white girls could be –
she was clueless, she was dumb, she ignored
the ways she wielded power
even as she claimed to refuse it –

she wore clogs and listened to National Public Radio;
she shopped only at farmer's markets; she considered monogamy
a function of capitalism – *and her insatiable drive to fuck poor people simply and obviously*
a symbol of humanitarianism – a way of spreading pleasure
to a people who really had none.

---

4 *post-script, broken-rulz:* baby would find real love for the first time in middle age after a series of failed encounters in sex & romance. *she had broken the rulz –* she was jobless, broke. she had one child who refused to speak to her, another who mooched off her small savings account with emotional blackmail so obvious that it made doctor goodall cringe that her client, baby, was in fact fifty-five years old and under the complete control of another baby, her own baby re: *give me da money mama! give me da money!* baby's daughter had demanded. yes, baby had found real grown-up love, a kind of love which made her bold and independent and kind, but she was still a child in so many ways, still infantilized by the false gods of a self-annihilating motherhood, still beholden to the belief that love meant submission.

she grabbed the tits & cock of those who were easy access,
those who she knew wouldn't fight back.

they didn't fight back. or then, maybe they did.　　　maybe they did, maybe?
maybe not?　　maybe they didn't because　　they couldn't?
maybe?　　　they could?
they were passive & limp –　　flimsy thin things; she drew in her breath.
she breathed.　　　　they scattered / like bits of tiny dust particles.

OR? Again – A Post-Apocalyptic-Script – THEN: a Limp Resurrection, an – Insurrection

the rulz of pleasure demanded baby be callous, cold;
she took pleasure but she gave none –

the rulz of money demanded baby exploit the bodies
of those she employed then enjoyed.

she didn't value them, she didn't love them.

it was a simple transaction; *cruelty was only the natural order of things –*
the rulz of money said so, said so plainly – plainly in Standard American English.

PROXIMATE VALUE:

"she was a profoundly jealous person."

"she was an angry person." "she was angry."
"she was homely."   "she had no home." [1]

"she was homeless." "she was homely & homeless." [2]

"she didn't know how to sell a book."

"she was frustrated by the fact that she was THIS kind of artist

and not THAT kind of artist."

"she was frustrated by the fact that she didn't know how to sell a book."

---

1 baby had loads of white girl guilt. she thought she might open a makeshift homeless shelter inside her apartment, she'd get the local Whole Foods Amazon to donate their leftovers, provided it was organic, provided it was fresh – provided it was *de-institutionalized, de-colonized, democratized!* baby thought she might offer the homeless folks pretty care packages – *goody bags!* – filled dark chocolate truffles, macadamia nuts, and tiny kumquats. Bernard, baby's first homeless friend, took a goody bag & poured its contents straight into his mouth. then he went to the bathroom to barf it all up.

2 baby thought empathy meant helping & aligning herself with all sorts of trendy lefty causes. *she wanted to have a place in heaven, goddamnit!* she wanted to pass through the pearly gates of heaven, she didn't want an ass whupping for *being baaaaad, for being so very baaaaad –*

"she was frustrated by the fact that she was bookless."

"she was frustrated." "she was sexually frustrated."

"she was frustrated by the fact that she might be forty and bookless."

"it wasn't about tenure."

"it wasn't about alimony."

"it wasn't about money."[3] "it wasn't about money."

"it was always about money." "it was always about money." "it wasn't about recognition."

"it was about her own dwindling self-respect, her own failure to achieve the goals

she'd set out to achieve."   "it was about goals."   "she had goals, god damn it."

"money wasn't the goal."[4] "money wasn't the goal." "believe me, money wasn't the goal."

---

3 baby knew homeless people were gross & homeless people were filthy, but she was also very much aware that the problem of homelessness was one of those intractable social problems – *which would only be solved by a cross-sector approach to urban decay and included – but was not beholden to – her own personal agency.* baby would write a version of this sentence in the sparkling pink brochure she would offer to visitors at Baby's Homeless Shelter Corporation.

4 baby first conceived of Baby's Homeless Shelter Corporation after she'd observed a homeless person camping outside her apartment. his name was Bernard, baby would learn. Bernard had a halo of fleas which circled his head and he carried a blanket stained with piss. she was disturbed by the scene, but she quickly got giddy as she dreamed of how she might fix it – *it would be easy!* she thought. *it would be simple* – she would open Baby's Homeless Shelter Corporation, which would offer an array of fine dining options – filet mignon, whole lobster, cornish hens cooked in truffle oil – each with chunky silver cutlery and gold-rimmed china plates. Baby's Homeless Shelter Corporation – the meals emphasized locally sourced ingredients and luxury rooms provided plush white bathrobes and five-foot jacuzzi for a people who generally had none. such amenities were classy – *and necessary* – and it would cure the homeless epidemic, baby believed.

"ok, ok." "ok."   "ok, then."

"she was goal-less." "she was -less."

"she was -less."

"she didn't realize this was entirely the point, this was entirely the project."

"she tried to name drop." "she tried to drop."

"she tried to name drop, she tried to drop a name."

"she dropped a name, she dropped a name."

"she dropped whose name?" "dropped whose drop?"

"name dropped whose drop?"

"she dropped whose name?" "she dropped a drop kick?"

"she drop kicked the name drop?"   "she wants to drop name droppings."

"she wants to drop the droppings."   "oh look, there are droppings."

"she wants to name the droppings."

"she wants to name drop the droppings."

"there are bird droppings on her hair."

"she wants to drop." "she wants to drop out."

"that's it – she wants to drop out."

"she wants[5] to drop out."

"she wants to drop out."

"she said it again." "she said it again & again."

"she wants to drop out."[6] "she wants to drop out."

"she tried to name drop." "she tried to name drop & then she dropped out."

"she couldn't name drop, so she dropped out."

"she dropped out because she name dropped."

"she dropped out and name dropped as she dropped out."

---

5   she wanted Baby's Homeless Shelter Corporation branded as an upscale bed and breakfast for the homeless, complete with thick, creamy napkins, cute blueberry muffins, whipped butter biscuits, and fresh squeezed orange juice each morning. she didn't understand that her first homeless friend, Bernard, did not enjoy living cramped between four walls, he was spooked by the arrangement, he thought himself too big for the intricate dining room table with long stemmed lilac flowers.

6   this was not the way. this was not the way. she didn't need to open up her home to bunch of dirty dope fiends who'd eventually rob & rape her and then continue on with their day, wandering the streets in bathrobes and long beards, resembling a pack of 8 charleston hestons – AKA 8 moseses – *blessed are the meek for they shall inherit the earth – lets bow our heads in prayer – bow our heads in prayer, goddddammmnnnniiiit –*

"it seemed a better option."

"it seemed a better sort of option."

"name drop as you drop out."

"drop out and name drop." "drop out and name drop."

"she dropped out, she couldn't name drop."

"she dropped out, she had no name."

"they dropped the name."

"they had no name."

"they had no name."

and then "voltron meets buns of steel"

the question was whether baby was *kinda-fat* or *fat-fat* –

& the distinction was one w/ch drove her starkly raving mad. how often did she stand on the scale, the little red ticker wavering slightly between 170 lbs & 171 lbs – and this was for our dear little girl – *baby* – who hovered somewhere near 5'6 and 5'6.34 – depending on whether or not she wore platforms – and whose exercise regime was not really *so* awful. (she played lacrosse in the spring, soccer in the fall, and sure – she had winters off but the gal was 14 and certainly no tara lipinsky.)

so baby was *kinda-fat* or *fat-fat* depending on the season (of sport) & the flavor (of cake). (she liked sheet cake from shaws w/ hot pink sprinkles & neon blue icing that snaked around the crown of the cake like a venomous tropical serpent.)

*

baby puked more often than not but could not get rid of that thick strip of chub that hung around her waist like a tool belt and puckered out of her skinny jeans, along with her *thong* – when she'd bend over or sit down or reach across the desk & attempt to make any sort of coy (re: lame) come-on to johnny t. walker, such as:

how'd you like to see my cup-cake (wink, wink)
or
wanna me to fetch you some skittles from the vending machine, sugar
or
hey mister athlete i love to play soccer & im really good with balls –

or

do you always make buttercream look so good

or

do you like buttercream biscuits (nudge, nudge)

or

hi blondie id like to share a secret w you if you don't mind

or sometimes she'd be a little more brazen:

ill give you a blowjob, behind the football field, underneath the bleachers at 17:55 PM –
be there or be square.

how johnny responded to these come-ons hovered somewhere between icy indifference and the
occasional concession. he did receive a blowjob from baby not once, but twice – though they
happened in the parking lot at 14:40/14:55 pm – behind ms. macintire's parked car after lacrosse
practice, two tuesdays in spring. for the most part, though, jonny t. looked at baby like the fat
pig she was and he'd occasionally *oink oink* at her in the hallways, especially if he was with his
teammates, a herd of football players who hung around him like hulking ox and would sometimes
grunt & make other indecipherable noises.

*

you better not say a fucking thing abt this bj baby – johnny t. said
       looking down at baby, her lips raw & round
around his long colonizer cock – *not a fucking thing.* she looked up at him w. big empty eyes &
nodded: uuuuhhhhhh huhhhh uhhhhh hhhhuhhhhh nottttt aaa fukkkkin ting not.afuk.in… ting.
nottttttttt.at.tttting.g.ggggnot-titt-tnoti-ttt-

SIX GRAMS OF DWORKIN

she critiqued herself, parroted herself nipped
    at her desire, clipped at it –

clipped at it this way and that way   with various questions – *yip, yip, yip*
    & then she nipped at his desire, nipped at his …

         [& then one day: *poooooooooffffff*   it was gone]

it was white feminists who critiqued her,
    it was white feminists who nipped – *nip, nip, nip* –
it was white feminists who bore holes

into her soul

white feminists who claimed they were doing it – *for her own good*
    they were doing it – *for her own liberation* –

white feminists were doing it because – *she couldn't save herself*
    she couldn't know herself –

& her own desires

she couldn't determine

  the moral value or not-value of the things she placed in her cunt –

a banana
a long-stemmed carrot, frozen
a tube of lipstick
a cigar
a finger, deformed
a pink plastic toy

& so desire would always be formed,
would always exist w. various holes in it

desire hung like a soft blanket w. big empty holes

where she had bitten out the parts that others loved most,

where she'd excised the parts of herself which made her who she was –

more clean & less queer

  more uppity & less unctuous

more jewey & less jappy

she did it because she thought they wanted it, she thought others wanted it
& she lived for others – *she discovered herself only through the eyes of others.*

what could she say, she was a wom-man

    she discovered herself only through the eyes of others –

"before it was nineteen seventy three"

      & the story of baby is this:
           & the story of baby is this: & the story of baby is this:

baby's mother had kicked her out after she'd discovered that baby liked ladies – and even w. baby's formidable accomplishments, even w. beating crack addiction, even w. beating alcohol – it was being gay that revolted her mother much more than anything else. sure, baby was a junkie who'd piss on the rug & steal grandmother's rubies; sure, she'd run her family into impossible debt; sure, she'd crammed sugar cookies into every nook & cranny of her body and stuck her finger down her throat in every bathroom from bedford hills to timbuktu. but lesbian? on top of every sin, mother could not possibly forgive the crime of lesbianism. it seemed a more virulent disease than anything else baby brought home – worse than herpes, worse than gonorrhea, worse than tooth decay. tongues & saliva & clitorises *w.o. the possibility of a penile erection* just seemed so wrong. it just seemed so foul. and so ...

w. in a few short days, mother had found crumpled panties, a dental dam, & baby's lover curled naked in bed ... & *whoooooosh* ... there she went ...
      & baby had landed herself on the streets.

*

      & the story of baby is this:
           & the story of baby is this: & the story of baby is this:

[*rewind 4 years earlier*]

*

each september the school nurse distributed 3 pamphlets to the schoolgirls,
at missus macintire's school for girls:

tips for mindful eating

　　　　　scoliosis: what you should know

& a short little primer called:

　　　　　baby's story

... *baby's story* read like a watered down version of a sex-ed video,

cast in a violet & violent hue. it spoke of the dark clouds that hung over a small town, where a
little girl named *baby* lived with a mother, father, and two little yapping dogs. one day the father
dies and two years later, a new father comes to town.

this new father is not all he's chalked up to be.

　　　baby is beaten & slapped
& pinched & poked
　　　& fucked & flipped inside and out.

baby read *baby's story* and concluded that little girls should be awfully afraid of their fathers,
step-fathers, uncles, mothers, brothers, and sisters.

they should not be afraid of their aunties –

aunties would not harm them. aunties were safe, safest of all.

& the story of baby is this:
        & the story of baby is this: & the story of baby is this:

[*rewind 2 years earlier*]

baby was 14 & popular (enough) & pretty (enough) & she seemed to have it all – she'd beaten
a difficult youth & she and her mother and her step-dad ray were living in a small apartment on
the west side of town. they'd wake up every morning & eat cheerios together, beginning their
day: mother would fry an egg, put carrots & ginger in the blender, maybe hand baby a brown-bag
lunch – and say "skitttttttttt-ddatle!" w. a grin as baby ran out each morning into the yellow sun.

                                        *

it was a ritual of sorts;
ray would knock on the door: *knock! knock! knock!*

baby would stay silent
& ray would turn the knob to find baby standing there, in the middle of the room, her body fixed
as a roman statue, swimming in the milky light of morning. ray would lift her arms up, peel off
her nightgown top & awkwardly throw it in the basket - he'd often miss. [pan out. cut to rumpled
knickers in basket.]

please wait until next Sunday when the final installment of "baby's story" concludes...

134

ABOUT THE AUTHOR
EL_S_TH H__ST_ON

ELISABETH HOUSTON WROTE AN AUTHOR BIOGRAPHY and then deleted said biography and then decided instead to write a paperback romance novel, which riffed off the prolific priestess of romance Miss Danielle Steel; this romance novel also required an encyclopedia to accompany its reading, a long thick index which contained towering columns of notes which distinguished facts from fiction, fiction from friction, words from gibberish, gibberish from poetry, and on and on. The books stalled at the final stages – printers got jammed, machines convulsed, ink and bodies and language run amok. Elisabeth Houston refused to write a proper author biography to be penned on the book's final page, and readers were tired and angry. Then the readers decided to riot. They demanded authorial integrity, they demanded coherence, and so they violently destroyed the book.